HELLENIC STUDIES 1

Plato's Rhapsody and Homer's Music:
The Poetics of the Panathenaic Festival in Classical Athens

Plato's Rhapsody and Homer's Music:
The Poetics of the Panathenaic Festival in Classical Athens

by

Gregory Nagy

Published by

Center for Hellenic Studies
Trustees for Harvard University
Washington, D.C.
and
Foundation of the Hellenic World
Athens, Greece

Distributed by Harvard University Press
Cambridge, Massachusetts, and London, England

2002

Plato's Rhapsody and Homer's Music: The Poetics of the Panathenaic Festival in Classical Athens
by Gregory Nagy

Copyright © 2002 Center for Hellenic Studies, Trustees for Harvard University.
All Rights Reserved.

Published by Center for Hellenic Studies, Trustees for Harvard University,
Washington, D.C. and Foundation of the Hellenic World, Athens, Greece

Distributed by Harvard University Press, Cambridge, Massachusetts and London,
England

Production and cover design: Athanasios Konstantopoulos

Cover Illustration: Detail, Nolan Amphora. Brygos Painter, 490-470 BCE. Boston,
Museum of Fine Arts.

Printed in Athens, Greece by Bibliosynergatiki SA

Library of Congress Cataloging-in-Publication Data
Nagy, Gregory.
    Plato's rhapsody and Homer's music : the poetics of the Panathenaic
Festival in classical Athens / Gregory Nagy.
        p. cm.
    Includes bibliographical references and index.
    ISBN 0-674-00963-0 (alk. paper)
        1. Homer--Literary style. 2. Epic poetry, Greek--History and criticism. 3. Athena
(Greek deity)--Cult--Greece--Athens. 4. Performing arts--Greece--Athens. 5. Athens
(Greece)--Civilization. 6. Oral tradition--Greece. 7. Oral-formulaic analysis. 8.
Transmission of texts. 9. Plato--Aesthetics. 10. Homer--Aesthetics. 11. Aesthetics,
Ancient. 12. Panathenaia. 13. Poetics. I. Title

PA 4175 .N34 2002
883'.01--dc21

                                                                    2002025737

ISBN 0-674-00963-0

The Foundation of the Hellenic World proudly presents *Plato's Homer and Homer's Music* as the first title in a new series of publications inaugurated in cooperation with Harvard University's Center for Hellenic Studies. It is only fitting that the first author in the series is Gregory Nagy, the Francis Jones Professor of Classical Greek Literature and Professor of Comparative Literature at Harvard University, and Director of the Center. Under Nagy's direction, the Center for Hellenic Studies has reaffirmed its commitment, as first articulated by its most distinguished founder, Paul Mellon, to take an active part in research on Greek civilization in the broadest sense of the word.

It is no accident that the subject of the first book is Homer. Today the need to rediscover the roots of Hellenic civilization is ever-present, and the study of Homer remains a vital starting point for this rediscovery, energizing and inspiring our own times.

For the Foundation of the Hellenic World, the new collaboration marks another step forward in its own outreach programs. One goal is to use new technologies to give prominence to the values and achievements of the past. For example, our Cultural Center, called "Hellenic Cosmos," is an innovative museum of Hellenism. Here visitors can experience Hellenic culture through a variety of modern technological tools and interactive exhibitions, such as three-dimensional reconstructions and virtual reality. Beyond the technology, however, our focus remains on academic research and thorough knowledge of the subject matter in order to maintain the highest aesthetic and historical standards.

It is our hope that the series will be a successful one and that it promotes the understanding of the past for the creation of a better future.

Lazaros Efraimoglou, President
Foundation of the Hellenic World

Table of Contents

Preface

This small book integrates the work that went into three pieces I published earlier on Plato's Homer (Nagy 1999b, 2000a, 2001a in the Bibliography). I thank the following for the advice they gave me: Alex Beecroft, Graeme Bird, Timothy Boyd, John McK. Camp, Miriam Carlisle, Derek Collins, Stamatia Dova, Casey Dué, Douglas Frame, Madeleine Goh, José González, John Hamilton, Albert Henrichs, Carolyn Higbie, Marianne Govers Hopman, Thomas Jenkins, Minna Skafte Jensen, Christopher Jones, Olga Levaniouk, Kevin McGrath, Leonard Muellner, Antonia Nagy, Blaise Nagy, László Nagy, Corinne Pache, Gloria Ferrari Pinney, Timothy Power, Karl Reichl, Kent Rigsby, and Samuel B. Seigle. They are not to be held responsible for any mistakes that may remain. I dedicate this book to the cherished Antonia, with fond memories of our many happy dialogues over Plato's skillful use of words.

Abbreviations in footnotes

BA/BA² *Best of the Achaeans* = N 1979/1999 [with preface]
GM   *Greek Mythology and Poetics* = N 1990b
HQ   *Homeric Questions* = N 1996b
HR   *Homeric Responses* = N 2002 (forthcoming)
PH   *Pindar's Homer* = N 1990a
PP   *Poetry as Performance* = N 1996a

Introduction

There is a pervasive historical connection, I argue in this book, between two evolving institutions—Homeric poetry and the festival of the Panathenaia in the city of Athens. The testimony of Plato will be crucial to the argumentation.

Two premises are involved. The first is this: synchronic approaches to Homer cannot succeed without the integration of diachronic approaches, just as diachronic approaches cannot succeed without the integration of the synchronic. The second premise is this: synchronic analysis of Homeric poetry can be successful only when that poetry is viewed as a *system* rather than a *text*. Short-hand, I refer to the system in question simply as "Homeric poetry." Testing these premises, I argue against the assumption that the Homeric text of the *Iliad* and *Odyssey*, as reconstituted in various editions both ancient and modern, is a single synchronic reality. In other words, I hold that the Homeric text (or texts) is not the same thing as Homeric poetry.[1]

In using the terms *synchronic* and *diachronic*, I follow a linguistic distinction made by Ferdinand de Saussure.[2] For Saussure, synchrony and diachrony designate respectively a current state of a language and a phase in its evolution.[3] I draw attention to Saussure's linking of *diachrony* and *evolution*, a link that proves to be crucial for understanding the medium that is central to this study, Homeric poetry. In my publications over the last twenty years, I have worked out a general "evolutionary model" for the oral traditions that shaped Homeric poetry.[4] This

---

[1] For further argumentation, see the Preface to N 1999a (2nd ed., hereafter abbreviated as *BA²*, updating the original N 1979 version, *BA*), p. xv.

[2] Saussure 1916:117.

[3] Saussure, ibid.: "De même *synchronie* et *diachronie* désigneront respectivement un état de langage et une phase d'évolution."

[4] See *BA²* xiv, with special reference to N 1996b (hereafter abbreviated as *HQ*) ch.2, "An Evolutionary Model for the Making of Homeric Poetry," pp. 29–63.

theory differs from various specific "dictation theories,"[5] not to mention various general assumptions about a "writing Homer."[6] In terms of my evolutionary model, the "making" of Homeric poetry needs to be seen diachronically as well as synchronically, if we follow Saussure's sense of diachrony.

Here I propose to add two restrictions to my use of *synchronic* and *diachronic*. First, I apply these terms consistently from the standpoint of an outsider who is thinking about a given system, not from the standpoint of an insider who is thinking within that system.[7] Second, I use *diachronic* and *synchronic* not as synonyms for *historical* and *current* respectively. Diachrony refers to the potential for evolution *in a structure*. History is not restricted to phenomena that are structurally predictable.[8]

With these working definitions in place, I return to my point: a purely synchronic perspective is insufficient for reading Homer. The transmitted texts of the Homeric *Iliad* and *Odyssey* cannot be reduced to single speech-events, self-contained in one time and one place, as if we had direct access to actual recordings of the language of Homer.[9] Not just the text but even the language of Homeric poetry resists a purely synchronic approach. The Homeric grammar and lexicon do not and cannot belong to any one time, any one place: in a word, they *defy synchronic analysis*.[10] In this connection, we need to confront the general phenomenon of *meaning* in the media of oral poetics. On

---

[5] I have in mind especially the theories of Janko (1982:191), Jensen (1980:92), and West (1990:34). My "evolutionary model" is not at odds, however, with the more general dictation theory of Lord 1953. See N 1998b. For polemics concerning another dictation theory, see N 1997d.

[6] More on these assumptions in *HA* 19, 27.

[7] *PH* 4.

[8] *PH* 21n18, following Jacopin 1988:35–36, who adds: "Both synchrony and diachrony are abstractions extrapolated from a model of reality." In N 1999b (also *HR*, Introduction), I offer a fuller discussion of the theoretical and practical problems connected with the terms synchronic / diachronic.

[9] Cf. *HQ* 17, 20.

[10] *GM* 29, with reference to the extended discussion in Householder and Nagy 1972:19–23.

the basis of my own cumulative work, I am convinced that *meaning* by way of *reference* in oral poetics needs to be seen diachronically as well as synchronically: each occurrence of a theme (on the level of content) or of a formula (on the level of form) in a given composition-in-performance refers not only to its immediate context but also to all other analogous contexts remembered by the performer or by any member of the audience.[11]

From a purely synchronic point of view, then, where can we find a sample of Homeric poetry, if not in the text of any single edition? The ideal sample would be an attested transcript of a "live" performance, which would amount to the recording of a "live" recomposition-in-performance. Of course, such a sample is for us an impossibility. Even "dictation theories" cannot claim an *attested* transcript: like all other theories, these too need to account for the lengthy manuscript tradition that fills the gap— between the time of the hypothesized archetype, that is, a dictated text, and the time of the earliest editions resulting from that tradition.[12]

Failing an ideal sample for synchronic analysis, we must resort to describing the system of Homeric poetry as reflected by Homeric textual transmission. But the point is, such description cannot be purely synchronic, in that the history of Homeric textual transmission cannot capture any single occasion of performance, any single occasion of recomposition-in-performance. All we can do is describe a *reconstructed* occasion, and such a description requires a diachronic as well as synchronic perspective.

In terms of my evolutionary model for the making of Homeric poetry, the goal is to reconstruct not only a single occasion but also a chronological sequence of occasions. With this goal in mind, I have worked out a tentative descriptive framework of five periods, "Five Ages of Homer," as it were:

---

[11] *PP* 50.

[12] For more on "dictation theories," see *HR*, Introduction.

(1) a relatively most fluid period, with no written texts, extending from the early second millennium into the middle of the eighth century in the first millennium BCE.

(2) a more formative or "pan-Hellenic" period, still with no written texts, from the middle of the eighth century to the middle of the sixth BCE.

(3) a definitive period, centralized in Athens, with potential texts in the sense of *transcripts*, at any of several points from the middle of the sixth century BCE to the later part of the fourth BCE; this period starts with the reform of Homeric performance traditions in Athens during the régime of the Peisistratidai.

(4) a standardizing period, with texts in the sense of transcripts or even *scripts*, from the later part of the fourth century to the middle of the second BCE; this period starts with the reform of Homeric performance traditions in Athens during the régime of Demetrius of Phalerum, which lasted from 317 to 307 BCE.

(5) a relatively most rigid period, with texts as *scripture*, from the middle of the second century BCE onward; this period starts with the completion of Aristarchus' editorial work on the Homeric texts, not long after 150 BCE or so, which is a date that also marks the general disappearance of the so-called "eccentric" papyri.[13]

There are different degrees of difficulty in attempting to reconstruct different occasions at different periods in the evolution of Homeric poetry. Needless to say, the difficulties increase exponentially as we move further back in time. Conversely, however, the difficulties decrease as we move forward in time,

---

[13] See *PP* 110 and the discussion in the pages that follow, with working definitions of the descriptive terms "transcript," "script," and "scripture." See also *HQ* 41, where the same descriptive scheme of five consecutive periods is more explicitly situated in an overall evolutionary model. The perspective on this scheme is different in the two analyses just cited: in *PP* 110 the analysis looks forward in time, while in *HQ* 41 it looks backward.

especially once we reach a point where the actual occasions of performance become historically verifiable. We reach such a point during what I call the third or "definitive" period in the scheme above, to be dated roughly to the middle of the sixth century BCE—and to be localized specifically in the city-state of Athens.

For the moment, we are looking at a possible point of contact between two of the three central subjects of this book, Homer and the festival of the Panathenaia in Athens. I seize this moment to connect the third central subject as well: Plato.

Why Plato? It is because he is our primary source of information about points of contact between Homer and the Panathenaia. Without Plato, the available evidence—literary, epigraphical, iconographical—is so meager that we might easily give up hope for reconstructing anything of significance. Even with Plato's help, the evidence is relatively meager. Still, we find in Plato references to Homer and the Panathenaia that are of great importance. Such references, both direct and indirect, are essential for my argumentation in developing an evolutionary model for the making of Homeric poetry.

I must stop at this point in order to stress a fundamental difference between my evolutionary model and other theories. My main argument is that the city of Athens in general and the Panathenaic Festival in particular can be viewed as two decisive historical factors in the gradual *shaping* of what became the definitive forms of the *Iliad* and *Odyssey*, starting with the sixth century BCE.[14] By contrast, those who accept the theory

---

[14] See *PP* 69–71, 77, 80–82, 111–112 (especially notes 21, 23, 24), 122–125, 143–144, 180n99, 189; *HQ* 42–43, 52, 69, 75, 80–81, 93–95, 100–111. See already *PH* 21–25 (especially p. 23), 28, 54, 71–73, 76, 104, 160–163 (with special reference to "Plato" *Hipparkhos* 228d), 191–192, 388n32, 391. I strongly agree with the historical perspectives of Seaford 1994, especially pp. 151–153 (with reference to *PH* 54, 71–73, 191–192 and to N 1992a:31, 41, 45–51). See also Cook 1995:5: "the crystallization of the Odyssean tradition into a written text, the growth of Athenian civic ritual, and the process of state formation in Attica were simultaneous and mutually reinforcing developments." See further Cook p. 145. For a pioneering work on questions of Homeric performances at the Panathenaia, see Jensen 1980.

of a so-called "Peisistratean Recension" assume that Athens in the sixth century provided a historical context merely for the *recording* of the Homeric poems as a fixed text.[15]

In pursuing my main argument, as I have just articulated it, I intend to examine systematically the overall testimony of Plato as an expert—albeit a hostile one—about the cultural legacy of Homeric performances at the Panathenaia.

---

[15] See, for example, S. West 1988:36, 39–40, 48, following Merkelbach 1952 (this work, though I distance myself from many of its assumptions, continues to be most useful for its comprehensive formulation of the theory). For a survey and critique of various forms of the theory of a "Peisistratean Recension," see *HQ* 99 and following.

Chapter 1
Homer and Plato at the Panathenaia[1]

By studying both direct and indirect references to the Panathenaia in the works of Plato, supplemented by occasional references in various other literary sources and in the attested epigraphical and iconographical evidence, we find opportunities for reconstructing what might be described as synchronic cross-sections or even "snapshots" of seasonally recurring occasions for the performing of Homeric poetry at the festival of the Panathenaia at Athens, dating back to at least as early as the sixth century BCE. A most useful starting-point is the *Hipparkhos* of "pseudo-Plato."[2] We are about to see a story that purports to explain an Athenian law requiring that the *Iliad* and *Odyssey* be performed *in sequence* by the *rhapsôidoi* 'rhapsodes' at the Panathenaia:

Ἱππάρχῳ ... ὃς ἄλλα τε πολλὰ καὶ καλὰ ἔργα σοφίας ἀπεδείξατο, καὶ τὰ Ὁμήρου ἔπη πρῶτος ἐκόμισεν εἰς τὴν γῆν ταυτηνί, καὶ ἠνάγκασε τοὺς ῥαψῳδοὺς Παναθηναίοις ἐξ ὑπολήψεως ἐφεξῆς αὐτὰ διιέναι, ὥσπερ νῦν ἔτι οἵδε ποιοῦσιν

Hipparkhos, ... who made a public demonstration of many and beautiful accomplishments to manifest his expertise [*sophia*], especially by being the first to bring over [*komizô*] to this land [= Athens] the poetic utterances [*epê*] of Homer, and he forced the rhapsodes [*rhapsôidoi*]

---

[1] The original version of this essay is N 1999b.

[2] The scholarly applications of the term "pseudo-" in the taxonomy of Classical authors can lead to misunderstandings. In this case, for example, it is important to keep in mind that the *Hipparkhos* is a genuine component of the Platonic tradition, even if the direct authorship of Plato has been questioned.

at the Panathenaia to go through [*diienai*] these utterances in sequence [*ephexês*], by relay [*hupolêpsis*], just as they [= the rhapsodes] do even nowadays.[3]

"Plato" *Hipparkhos* 228b–c

I draw special attention to two words with rhapsodic implications: *ephexês* 'in sequence' and *hupolêpsis*, which I translate as 'relay'. In dramatized dialogue, the corresponding verb of *hupolêpsis*, *hupolambanô*, marks the response of one speaker to the previous speaker: *ephê hupolabôn* 'he said in response' (e.g. Plato *Republic* I 331d, etc.; cf. Herodotus 1.11.5, 1.27.4, etc.). In Aristotle *Politics* V 1310a10, *hupolambanô* is correlated with *hupokrinomai* 'reply, make answer'.[4] As for *ephexês auta diienai* 'go through them [= the *epê* 'poetic utterances' of Homer] in sequence', we may compare the contexts of Plato *Timaeus* 23d3–4 / 24a1–2: *panta ... hexês dielthein / ephexês diienai* 'go through everything in sequence' / 'go through in sequence'.[5]

If we supplement this passage from the *Hipparkhos* with a passage taken from a speech delivered by the Athenian statesman Lycurgus (330 BCE), we may infer that the Homeric *epê* 'poetic utterances' performed at the Panathenaia were the *Iliad* and *Odyssey*:

---

[3] General commentary on the whole passage in *HQ* 80–81.

[4] In LSJ, meaning II of *hupokrinomai* is given as '*speak in dialogue*, hence *play a part* on the stage,' as in Demosthenes 19.246, where the part played is in the accusative: τὴν Ἀντιγόνην Σοφοκλέους ... ὑποκέκριται 'has played the part of Sophocles' *Antigone*'. Here and elsewhere, I use single rather than double quotation marks whenever I print translations of the original Greek.

[5] In the chapter that follows, I argue that Plato is using rhapsodic metaphors in these contexts of the *Timaeus*. When it is Critias' turn in the *Critias* to take up where Timaeus in the *Timaeus* had left off, Timaeus refers to the *hexês logos* 'continuous discourse' that they had agreed upon (*Critias* 106b7). When Critias actually starts speaking, he uses the word *dekhomai* (106b8). For the rhapsodic sense of 'I take up where you (/ he / they) left off', see my discussion of *Iliad* IX 191 below.

βούλομαι δ᾽ ὑμῖν καὶ τὸν "Ομηρον παρασχέσθαι ἐπαινῶν. οὕτω γὰρ ὑπέλαβον ὑμῶν οἱ πατέρες σπουδαῖον εἶναι ποιητήν, ὥστε νόμον ἔθεντο καθ᾽ ἑκάστην πενταετηρίδα τῶν Παναθηναίων μόνου τῶν ἄλλων ποιητῶν ῥαψῳδεῖσθαι τὰ ἔπη, ἐπίδειξιν ποιούμενοι πρὸς τοὺς "Ελληνας ὅτι τὰ κάλλιστα τῶν ἔργων προῃροῦντο.

I wish to adduce[6] for you Homer, <u>quoting [epaineô]</u> him,[7] since the <u>reception</u>[8] that he had from your ancestors made him so important a poet that there was a law enacted by them that requires, every fourth year of the Panathenaia, the <u>rhapsodic performing [rhapsôideô]</u> of his <u>poetic utterances [epê]</u>—his alone and no other poet's. In this way they [= your ancestors] made a <u>demonstration</u>

---

[6] The orator Lycurgus, by 'adducing' the classical authors (I mean "classical" from his synchronic point of view), assumes the role of statesman. This point will be developed further in the analysis that follows.

[7] To make his arguments here in *Against Leokrates* 102, the orator is about to adduce a 'quotation' from Homer, the equivalent of what we know as *Iliad* Book XV verses 494–499. On my working translation 'quote' for *epaineô*, see the analysis below. Adducing a Homeric 'quotation' is presented here as if it were a matter of adducing Homer himself. In the same speech, at an earlier point, Lycurgus (*Against Leokrates* 100) had quoted 55 verses from Euripides' *Erekhtheus* (fr. 50 Austin). At a later point (*Against Leokrates* 107), he quotes 32 verses from Tyrtaeus (fr. 10 West), whom he "patriotically" identifies as an Athenian (so also Plato *Laws* I 629a). On the politics and poetics of the Athenian appropriation of Tyrtaeus *and* of his poetry, see *GM* 272–273. I suggest that the Ionism of poetic diction in the poetry of Tyrtaeus can be explained along the lines of an evolutionary model of rhapsodic transmission: see *PH* 53, 434 (cf. also *HQ* 111); see also *PH* 23n27 on Lycurgus *Against Leokrates* 106–107, where the orator mentions a customary law at Sparta concerning the performance of the poetry of Tyrtaeus.

[8] I deliberately translate *hupolambanô* 'receive' here in terms of "reception theory." In terms of rhapsodic vocabulary, as we saw above in "Plato" *Hipparkhos* 228b–c, *hupolêpsis* is not just 'reception' but also 'continuation' in the sense of reception by way of relay.

[*epideixis*],[9] intended for all Hellenes to see,[10] that they made a conscious choice of the most noble of accomplishments.[11]

Lycurgus *Against Leokrates* 102[12]

According to the story in "Plato" *Hipparkhos,* as quoted earlier, we see that there existed in Athens a custom of maintaining a fixed narrative sequence of Homeric performance at the Panathenaia, with each performing rhapsode taking up the narration where the previous rhapsode left off. Classicists conventionally refer to this custom as the "Panathenaic Rule."[13] The author of the *Hipparkhos* says that this custom was initiated by Hipparkhos, son of Peisistratos, in the era of the tyrants. There are those who view this story as the reflex of a historical event, estimating the date at around 530 BCE.[14]

---

[9] Cf. the context of *epideigma* 'display, demonstration' in "Plato" *Hipparkhos* 228d, as discussed in *PH* 161; cf. also *id.* pp. 217 and following on *apodeixis* 'presentation, demonstration'. The basic idea behind what is being 'demonstrated' is a *model for performance.*

[10] By implication, the pan-Hellenic impulse of the 'ancestors' of the Athenians in making Homer a "Classic" is mirrored by the impulse of Lycurgus, statesman that he is, to 'quote' extensively from such "Classics" as Homer, Tyrtaeus, and Euripides. See also "Plutarch" *Lives of the Ten Orators* 841f on the initiatives taken by Lycurgus to produce a "State Script" of the dramas of Aeschylus, Sophocles, and Euripides (commentary in *PP* 174–175, 189n6, 204).

[11] I infer that the *erga* 'accomplishments' include poetic accomplishments: on the mentality of seeing a reciprocity between noble deeds and noble poetry that becomes a deed in celebrating the deed itself, see *PH* 70, 219.

[12] Further discussion of this passage: *PH* 21–24.

[13] Davison 1955:7. Cf. *HQ* 75, 81–82, 101.

[14] Davison 1968:60; cf. Shapiro 1992:72–75. See also Kotsidu 1991:41–44. Even if the Panathenaic Rule were to be viewed in terms of a single historical moment centering on the political initiatives of Hipparkhos, it is a given that the institution of rhapsodic competitions at the Panathenaia predates such a theoretical moment. Note the formulation of Shapiro 1993:101–103: "performances by rhapsodes at the Panathenaia did take place before Hipparkhos introduced the so-called Panathenaic Rule." He cites as evidence the depiction of a rhapsode on a black-figure Liverpool amphora of Panathenaic shape, dated to ca. 540 BCE (see his figures 26 and 27).

My own analysis does not rule out the possibility that such a reported event was a historical fact—to the extent that an important political figure like Hipparkhos may well have reformed the custom of epic performances at the Panathenaia.[15] But I insist that there are two far more basic historical facts to be inferred from the story: (1) the author of the *Hipparkhos* says that this custom of relay performances of Homer by rhapsodes at the Panathenaia *was still in effect during his own lifetime* and (2) the custom is described in terms of a customary law, instituted by Hipparkhos in the role of a "lawgiver."[16]

It is also a historical fact, I argue, that the Peisistratidai in general, most notably the father of Hipparkhos, Peisistratos himself, appropriated to themselves the role of "lawgiver," and that stories of the so-called "Peisistratean Recension" fit a larger pattern of myths about lawgivers as culture heroes who institutionalized Homeric poetry in their own respective city-states.[17] This is not the place to survey the stories about the "Peisistratean Recension" in terms of an evolutionary model for the making of Homeric poetry—a task that I have undertaken elsewhere.[18] Here I seek only to situate the story about the Panathenaic Rule, as quoted above from "Plato" *Hipparkhos* 228b–c, within the larger context of other such stories—and within a broader historical perspective that views the applications and reapplications of myths about lawgivers as an ever-evolving political process.

In another version of the story that explains the ongoing custom of relay performances of Homer by rhapsodes at the Panathenaia, the Panathenaic Rule was supposedly instituted by the lawgiver Solon:

---

[15] *HQ* 74, 80–81.
[16] On myths about lawgivers as founders of customary laws, see the discussion in *GM* 21, 71–75, 81, 102, 105.
[17] Extensive discussion in *HQ* 71–75, 78, 103.
[18] *HQ* 67, 70, 74, 93–96, 99–104.

τά τε Ὁμήρου ἐξ ὑποβολῆς γέγραφε ῥαψῳδεῖσθαι, οἷον ὅπου ὁ πρῶτος ἔληξεν, ἐκεῖθεν ἄρχεσθαι τὸν ἐχόμενον

He [= Solon the Lawgiver] has written a law that the works of Homer are to be performed rhapsodically [*rhapsôideô*], by relay [*hupobolê*],[19] so that wherever the first person left off, from that point the next person should start.

Dieuchidas of Megara FGH 485 F 6
via Diogenes Laertius 1.57[20]

According to my analysis, this version represents a post-sixth-century political reapplication of the mythology that motivates the Panathenaic Rule. This time, the political perspective is that of democratic Athens in the era after the tyrants, and thus the "lawgiver" credited with the ongoing custom of performing Homeric poetry at the Panathenaia of Athens is no longer Hipparkhos (or Peisistratos) but Solon, the culture hero of the Athenian democracy. The same kind of political mentality is evident in the wording of the Lycurgus passage quoted above, where the "ancestors" of the Athenians are said to have "passed a law," νόμον ἔθεντο—in the best democratic tradition imaginable.

From a diachronic perspective, then, I suggest that both the Peisistratean and Solonian versions of stories concerning the Panathenaic Rule have a historical validity, to the extent that both of the different versions could provide, in different

---

[19] My translation of *hupobolê* as 'relay' will be explained in the discussion that follows.

[20] For more on Dieuchidas of Megara (FGH 485 F 6), see Merkelbach 1952:24–25. Dieuchidas has been variously dated to the 4th or the 3rd/2nd century BCE (see the bibliography in Figueira 1985:118 par. 9n2; the bibliography in S. West 1988:37n14 needs to be corrected).

historical periods, a coherent aetiology for the evolving institution of rhapsodic performances of Homer at the Panathenaia. It is needless to assume, as some do, that one or the other version of the story must come closer to what really happened, as it were.[21]

The variant narratives in "Plato" *Hipparkhos* 228b–c and Dieuchidas of Megara FGH 485 F 6 (via Diogenes Laertius 1.57) concerning the Panathenaic Rule are central to my evolutionary model for the making of Homeric poetry.[22] Both versions of the story are of great historical importance, since they take it as a given that the Homeric *Iliad* and *Odyssey* are a unity, an integral whole, and that this unity is connected with rhapsodic sequencing, an institution evidently still current in the era of the author of the *Hipparkhos*.[23] As we have seen, the actual idea of sequencing is marked by the adverb *ephexês* 'in sequence', as in "Plato" *Hipparkhos* 228c. According to the logic of these narratives, the unity of Homeric *composition* is a result of rhapsodic sequencing in *performance*.[24]

It is facile to assume that the Panathenaic Rule became a reality only when the performing rhapsodes had a written "script" that they could memorize. Granted, I do not rule out the possibility that rhapsodes had access, even as early as the sixth

---

[21] Cf. Davison 1968:58–59 and S. West 1988:37.

[22] With specific reference to "Plato" *Hipparkhos* 228b–c, I say already in 1990 (*PH* 23): "even if the size of either the *Iliad* or the *Odyssey* ultimately defied performance by any one person at any one sitting, the monumental proportions of these compositions could evolve in a social context where the sequence of performance, and thereby the sequence of narrative, could be regulated, as in the case of the Panathenaia." See also *HQ* 80–85.

[23] I agree with Boyd 1994:115 when he argues: "neither pseudo-Plato nor Diogenes Laertius [Dieuchidas of Megara FGH 485 F 6] states that a *text* is to be recited in order, but rather that the *rhapsodes* are to recite in order." But I disagree with his further argument, that the *content* of what the rhapsodes performed did not have to be in order. I also disagree with his argument that the term *hupobolê* mentioned in Diogenes Laertius 1.57 is to be understood in terms of a "cue" given by the judges to signal merely the taking of turns from one rhapsode's performance to another's. As I will argue below, *hupobolê* involves content as well as form.

[24] *HQ* 81.

century BCE ("period 3"), to transcripts of Homeric performances.[25] But the point is, I resist the assumption that the rhapsodic tradition required such a text. To assume that the rhapsodes performing at the Panathenaia needed a Homeric text is to undervalue the phenomenon of rhapsodic sequencing as I have just described it.

Rhapsodic sequencing is linked to another phenomenon, "relay mnemonics." This phenomenon is attested already in Homeric poetry, and I propose here to analyze two attestations. On the basis of these examples, I hope to show that relay mnemonics is a principle that links the Homeric and the rhapsodic traditions—from a diachronic perspective.

The *Iliad* gives a stylized representation of relay mnemonics in the scene where Achilles is shown performing the epic songs of heroes, *klea andrôn* 'glories of men' at *Iliad* IX 189, while Patroklos is waiting for his own turn, in order to take up the song precisely where Achilles will have left off (verb *lêgô* 'leave off'):

τὸν δ' εὗρον φρένα τερπόμενον φόρμιγγι λιγείῃ
καλῇ δαιδαλέῃ, ἐπὶ δ' ἀργύρεον ζυγὸν ἦεν,
τὴν ἄρετ' ἐξ ἐνάρων πόλιν Ἠετίωνος ὀλέσσας·
τῇ ὅ γε θυμὸν ἔτερπεν, ἄειδε δ' ἄρα <u>κλέα ἀνδρῶν</u>.
<u>Πάτροκλος</u> δέ οἱ <u>οἶος</u> ἐναντίος ἧστο σιωπῇ,
<u>δέγμενος</u> Αἰακίδην <u>ὁπότε λήξειεν ἀείδων</u>

And they [the members of the embassy] found him [Achilles] delighting his spirit with a clear-sounding lyre,
beautiful and well-wrought, and there was a silver bridge on it.

16

He won it out of the spoils after he destroyed the city of
Eetion.
Now he was delighting his spirit with it, and he sang the
glories of men [klea andrôn].[26]
But Patroklos, all alone, was sitting, facing him, in
silence,
waiting for whatever moment the Aeacid [Achilles]
would leave off [lêgô] singing.

Iliad IX 184–191

I offer the following analysis of this passage:

So long as Achilles alone sings the *klea andrôn* 'glories
of men', these heroic glories cannot be heard by anyone
but Patroklos alone. Once Achilles leaves off and
Patroklos starts singing, however, the continuum that is
the *klea andrôn*—the Homeric tradition itself—can at
long last become activated. This is the moment awaited
by *Patrokleês* 'he who has the *klea* [glories] of the ancestors'. In this Homeric image of Patroklos waiting for his
turn to sing, then, we have in capsule form the esthetics
of rhapsodic sequencing.[27]

---

26 On *kleos* (plural *klea*) in the sense of heroic glory as conferred by song, see N 1974,
especially pp. 244–252. The counter-arguments of Olson 1995:224–227 are, I think,
unsuccessful, as I argue in N 2000d (also in *HR*). I note here in passing that Olson's
approach is lacking in diachronic perspective.
27 *PP* 72–73. Cf. Ford 1992:115n31, who notes the use of *lêgô* 'leave off' at the point
in the narrative where Demodokos leaves off his Trojan narrative (*Odyssey* viii 87);
this verb, Ford argues, "is the technical expression used by a rhapsode to end a performance or a part of one." For parallels, he cites *Homeric Hymn to Dionysus* 17–18,
Hesiod fr. 305.4 MW, and *Theogony* 48. He also cites Diogenes Laertius 1.57
[Dieuchidas of Megara FGH 485 F 6], already cited by me above, and the line from
the *Iliad* (IX 191) that is presently under discussion. On this line, he refers to the analysis by Dunkel 1979:268–269 (*lêgô* is "used of poetic competition").

In terms of this argument, Homeric poetics is already a matter of rhapsodic poetics—from an evolutionary point of view. Understanding "evolution" in the broader sense of explicitly including history as well as diachrony, I have already spoken of an "evolutionary model" for the making of Homeric poetry. A subset of this model is my argument for the evolution of the formal medium of this poetry, dactylic hexameter.[28] Another subset of this model is my argument for the evolution of the mediators of this medium, the rhapsodes:

> In terms of my evolutionary model for the making of Homeric poetry, the figure of the rhapsode [*rhapsôidos*] is the very embodiment of an evolving medium that continues, in the course of time, to put more and more limitations on the process of recomposition-in-performance. The succession of rhapsodes linking a Homer in the remote past with Homeric performances in the "present" of the historical period—as extrapolated from such accounts as Plato's *Ion*—is a *diachronic* reality. This reality can only be distorted by any attempt to arrive at a *synchronic* definition of rhapsodes, meant as some kind of foil for an idealized definition of Homer.[29]

So far, I have argued that the principle of relay mnemonics, as represented in the first of the two Homeric examples, fuels the dynamics of rhapsodic sequencing: each rhapsode waits for his turn to pick up the narrative where the previous rhapsode left off. I will now argue that relay mnemonics involves not only rhapsodic sequencing but also rhapsodic competition, and that the mechanism of the rhapsodic relay is by nature competitive. While the element of competition is only implicit in the first

---

[28] See *PH*, specifically invoking the term *evolve / evolutionary* at pp. 11, 18, 21, 23–24, 53–54, 56–58, 82–82, 191, 196–198, 360, 415.

[29] *HQ* 82.

Homeric example that we have seen, it is explicit in the second example that we are about to see, which features the words *hupoblêdên* and *hupoballô* in two passages that I relate with one another in terms of these words. I propose that these words, the meanings of which are not clear to us in their Homeric attestations, reflected the technical language of the rhapsodes.

Before we turn to this second Homeric example, let us review the report of Dieuchidas of Megara (FGH 485 F 6 via Diogenes Laertius 1.57) about the Panathenaic Rule, which requires that the poetry of Homer "be performed rhapsodically [*rhapsôideô*], by relay [*ex hupobolês*], so that wherever the first person left off, from that point the next person should start." My translation of *hupobolê* as 'relay' is at odds with the definition in the LSJ dictionary, which gives 'prompt' or 'cue'.[30] These translations are based on such contexts as in Plutarch *Precepts of Statecraft* 814f, where actors in a theater are described as τοῦ ... ὑποβολέως ἀκούοντας 'listening to the *hupoboleus*'. Granted, the *hupoboleus* here is the practical equivalent of 'prompter' in theatrical terms, but I contend that the more basic function of the *hupoboleus,* in rhapsodic terms, is that of the continuator, the maintainer of the relay principle, the one who keeps the sequence going from the point where one actor's "lines" end and another actor's "lines" begin.

The translation of the rhapsodic term *hupobolê* as 'relay' meshes with the Homeric usage of *hupoballô* and *hupoblêdên*. Let us start with an Iliadic passage featuring the word *hupoballô*:

ἑσταότος μὲν καλὸν ἀκουέμεν οὐδὲ ἔοικεν
ὑββάλλειν, χαλεπὸν γάρ, ἐπιστάμενόν περ ἐόντα

---

[30] LSJ p. 1876 s.v. *hupobolê* I 3, where this passage is discussed (with cross-references to p. 1875 s.v. *hupoballô* III; also to p. 1876 s.v. *hupoblêdên* and p. 1887 s.v. *hupolêpsis*).

It is a good thing to listen to one who is standing, and it
is unseemly
to *hupoballein* him, for it is difficult to do so, even for
one who is expert.

Iliad XIX 79–80

Agamemnon is here speaking publicly to the assembly of war-
riors while remaining in a seated position (verse 77), saying that
it is a good thing to listen to a man who speaks in a standing position and that it is difficult for even a good speaker to *hupoballein*
him (ὑββάλλειν, verse 80). Achilles had just spoken to the
assembly at verses 56–73, and verse 55 makes it explicit that *he*
was standing.

The definition of *hupoballô* in LSJ (p. 1875 s.v.), with
specific reference to this passage, is "'suggest, whisper', as a
prompter does"; building on this definition, the dictionary
arrives at the interpretation 'interrupt' for *hupoballô* here, following the suggestion of the B scholia to *Iliad* XIX 80.
Accordingly, one commentator interprets *Iliad* XIX 79–80 as
follows: "It is good to listen *to someone who is standing up* <as
Achilles was, whom you have just applauded; but I cannot
stand, because of my wound>."[31] This commentator, who
accepts the interpretation of this compound verb *hupoballô* as
'interrupt', goes on to say: "The only other use of this compound in the sense of 'interrupt' was the *hapax* ὑποβλήδην
(*hupoblêdên*) at [*Iliad* I] 292, where Achilles rudely interrupted
Agamemnon in the final exchange of the quarrel."[32] Another
commentator translates ὑποβλήδην (*hupoblêdên*) at *Iliad* I 292
as "interruptingly."[33]

---

[31] Edwards 1991:244.
[32] Edwards p. 244.
[33] Kirk 1985:82.

I agree with the two commentators' general interpretations of these two Iliadic passages, at least in terms of the short-range meanings that they read into these passages, but I disagree with their specific interpretations of *hupoblêdên* / *hupoballein* as 'interruptingly' / 'interrupt'. Here I apply the work of Richard Martin on the performative aspect of Homeric "quotations" of heroes' speeches.[34] As Martin has shown in detail, the speeches of Achilles and Agamemnon and other epic characters are not only "quoted" by epic performance: they become part of the epic performances, and the speakers thus become performers in their own right.[35]

At *Iliad* I 292, Achilles engages in verbal combat with Agamemnon not so much by "interrupting" but by picking up the train of thought exactly where his opponent left off—and out-performing him in the process. At *Iliad* XIX 80, Agamemnon backs off from verbal combat with Achilles, using his wound as an excuse: I can't stand up, and therefore I can't compete by picking up the train of thought where Achilles left off—and therefore I can't out-perform him (and perhaps I don't anymore have the stomach even to try to do so).[36] The successful performer remains standing, and the unsuccessful performer fails to stand up and compete by taking his turn, choosing instead to sit it out. He will still speak, but he will speak without offering any more competition. We could explore at much greater length the implications of Achilles' besting of Agamemnon not only as hero but also as performer—and thereby insuring the perpetuity of the

<hr>

[34] Martin 1989.

[35] Cf. Martin 1989:117, with reference to the speech of Agamemnon as dramatized in *Iliad* XIX 78–144. Note Martin's formulation at p. 220: "Speaking to win out—this is the goal of every Iliadic performer."

[36] On the out-performing of Agamemnon by Achilles, see Martin 1989:63, 69–70, 98, 113, 117, 119, 133, 202, 219, 223, 228. See especially p. 141, a discussion of *Iliad* XXIII 657, 706, 752, 801, 830, where Achilles stands up to speak five times. Also p. 116: "Instead of promising *kleos* ..., the faulty speaker [that is, Agamemnon] must hold out material reward only." Also p. 198: "[Achilles] will go on to defeat Agamemnon, symbolically, by being the best performer on the verbal level" (cf. p. 223).

epic performance tradition that glorifies him, that gives him *kleos* and is *kleos*. What matters most for the moment is simply that the competition between Achilles and Agamemnon as performers takes place within the framework of a narrative continuum. The principle of relay mnemonics, to repeat, is to compete in the process of maintaining an overall continuum.

Such a principle is evident in Plato's *Ion*. This dialogue is named after a rhapsode from Ephesus who comes to Athens to compete for first prize at the Panathenaia (καὶ τὰ Παναθήναια νικήσομεν, *Ion* 530b2). Plato's wording makes it explicit that the occasion for the performing of Homer by rhapsodes at the Panathenaia is in effect a *competition* or *contest* among rhapsodes, an *agôn* (ἀγῶνα at *Ion* 530a5, picked up by ἠγωνίζου and ἠγωνίσω at a8), and that the agonistic art of the *rhapsôidoi* 'rhapsodes' falls under the general category of *mousikê* (μουσικῆς at a7). Similarly in Isocrates *Panegyricus* 159 the wording specifies that *Homeric* performances were taking place "in contests of *mousikê*," ἐν τοῖς μουσικοῖς ἄθλοις.[37]

In light of the fact that the Panathenaic event of Homeric performances by rhapsodes is designated by ancient sources in terms of an *agôn* or an *athlon*, both words meaning 'competition' or 'contest', we can see that there are really two aspects of the Panathenaic Rule: not only must the rhapsodes take turns as they perform the *Iliad* and *Odyssey* in sequence, they must also compete with each other in the process.[38]

The rhapsode Ion performs Homer not only on such major occasions as the competitions taking place at the festival of the Panathenaia. He also performs Homer on less formal occasions such as the convivial but competitive encounter dramatized in Plato's dialogue *Ion*, where we see the rhapsode being challenged by Socrates to perform a given selection from the Homeric *Iliad* and *Odyssey*.

---

37 See *PP* 111n24.
38 I confront for the first time this aspect of rhapsodic performance in *PH* 23–24n28.

The term "selection" is misleading, however. It implies a purely textual mentality—as if all that Ion had to do was to "quote" some passage that he had read and happened to have memorized. Even the word "quote" can mislead, since it could imply *the saying of words that have already been written*. In my own discussion, I continue to use "quote" only in a restricted sense, to mean *the saying of words that have already been spoken*. To signal this semantic restriction, I will continue to use the word "quote" only in quotes, in order to stress that I mean no implications of textuality. In the art of the rhapsode, to "quote" is not to "take" something out of a text, out of context. The rhapsodic "taking" of words requires the mnemonics of continuity.[39] What the rhapsode can do is to *start anywhere* in the *Iliad* and *Odyssey* and, once started, to *keep going*.

When Ion is challenged by Socrates to narrate the advice of Nestor to Antilokhos on the occasion of the Funeral Games for Patroklos (*Ion* 537a5–7), the rhapsode straightway launches into what we—in our own current scholarly synchronism—understand to be *Iliad* Book XXIII verses 335 and following. The wonder of it all is that the rhapsode knows exactly where to start. Starting off, he proceeds *in medias res*. Not only that: he evidently has the power to continue the narrative in an open-ended way, going on and on until there is some reason—internal or external—for him to stop. Socrates recognizes this early on, and he puts on the brakes before Ion gets too far into the narrative, calling out to the rhapsode: ἀρκεῖ 'that's enough!' (537c1).[40] The rhapsode has not yet gone very far, reaching what we know as *Iliad* Book XXIII verse 340, but the point has already been made: Ion has already proved himself to be a virtuoso rhapsode with phenomenal powers of "relay mnemonics."

---

[39] I am using "take" here in the sense of ἔνθεν ἑλὼν 'taking it from the point where …' at *Odyssey* viii 500 referring to the point of departure for the narration of Demodokos when he sings the story of the Trojan Horse. The narration starts *in medias res*.

[40] Cf. Murray 1996:127.

In his own turn, Socrates will make his own point. Plato's flow of narrative will provide Socrates with the arguments he needs to undermine Ion's defense of the rhapsode's art or *tekhnê*. The Homeric content of what Ion has already performed gives Socrates ammunition for his own argumentation. In other words, Socrates actually draws on Homeric performance in order to make his argument. As we shall see in a moment, rhapsodes argue this way themselves.[41]

Not to be outdone in anything by Ion, Socrates then proceeds to show off his own rhapsodic skills. He argues against Ion's arguments by likewise "quoting" Homer and then by engaging in a verbal commentary on his "quotations." In order to "quote" Homer, Socrates performs Homer rhapsodically in his own right, since he too joins Homer midstream—but he does it at three different points of the narrative. In rapid succession, Socrates "quotes" a series of Homeric "passages" in order to out-argue Ion—and even to out-perform him rhapsodically (538d1–3, 539a1–b1, 539b4–d1).[42]

As we see from the *Ion*, then, you can tell a rhapsode where to start performing Homer just by telling him what part of the narrative you want to hear, and you can count on him to start right there. The rhapsode's cue is not a matter of text: it is a matter of mnemonics. You cue him by giving him an idea, and that idea translates immediately into a specific point within the "stream of consciousness" that *is* the narrative flow of Homer— let us call it Homer's narrative consciousness. I will argue in a moment that the rhapsodes have a word for Homer's consciousness—*dianoia*. As we will see, a key passage is the beginning of

---

[41] Cf. already *PP* 123–124, with reference to Isocrates *Panathenaicus* 18–19 and 33.

[42] For commentary on the formal variations between the Homeric verses as transmitted in the medieval vulgate and the Homeric verses as quoted in the Platonic textual traditions, see Murray 1996:126 and 128. On Plato's "text" of Homer as an indirect reflex of Panathenaic performance traditions in the 5th and 4th centuries BCE, see *PP* 142–146.

Plato's *Ion*. For now, however, let me just dwell a bit further on the simple wonder of it all: the rhapsode has—or thinks he has—complete access to Homer's stream of consciousness, to Homer's authorial intent. By implication, the rhapsode will argue with you by joining Homer midstream at exactly the point where Homer will help him make an argument against you.

We see here the virtuosity of *making mental connections in a competitive situation,* that is, in an *agôn.* The rhapsode's mind, I argue, is trained to connect, to make associations: the rhapsodic competitions at festivals like the Panathenaia require his readiness to take up the narrative where a competing rhapsode has left off. If this argument holds, we have here the essence of the principle of relay mnemonics in the art or *tekhnê* of the rhapsode. The driving force of relay mnemonics is competition.

In the staged dialogue of the *Ion*, Plato's fine-tuned ear for language—not just any language but in this case the technical language of high-class artisans like rhapsodes—has I think picked up on a variety of authentic expressions and turns of phrase that echo the talk of real rhapsodes as they once upon a time practiced their art or *tekhnê*—and even as they once upon a time *spoke about* this real *tekhnê.* I have collected ten examples:

1. *hormaô* + accusative, in the sense of 'get [the performer] started, inspire': 534c3. Plato's ear catches the technical nature of this word, and he uses it in a technical context: the Muse 'inspires' various different kinds of poet to produce their various different kinds of poetry. On the surface, Plato makes it look as if only composition is involved, not performance: in the context of 534c, the Muse 'inspires' Homer to make epic, just as she 'inspires' other poets to make dithyrambs, encomia, and so on. The Homeric context of the word *hormaô*, however, makes it clear that inspiration by the Muse happens in the context of performance, and it has to happen from the very start: the Muse has to 'start' the performer. At *Odyssey* viii 499, we see the blind singer Demodokos about to start his performance: *hormêtheis*

theou arkheto (ὁρμηθεὶς θεοῦ ἄρχετο) 'getting started, he began with the god'. That is, the performer got started or 'inspired' by the Muse and then he began his performance, starting by hymning a god. What follows this start, as we hear it paraphrased by the *Odyssey*, is an epic account of the Iliou Persis, the destruction of Troy (viii 500–520). (In terms of the narrative chronology of the overall narrative tradition culminating in the destruction of Troy, the performative 'start' here is situated near the compositional 'conclusion'.) The wording **hormêtheis** 'getting started' at viii 499 has to do with the singer's point of departure: the verb *hormaô* is derived from the noun **hormê**, aptly described as "le seul véritable dérivé de *ornumi*";[43] *hormê* can mean 'setting oneself in motion', as at the start of a march (LSJ s.v., III); I note the compound **aphormê**, which actually means 'point of departure' (cf. *aphormêthentos* at *Iliad* II 794, *Odyssey* ii 375, iv 748).

2. **âidô** 'narrate' (= 'sing') + accusative of a given topic, which must be named at the very beginning of the performance. The topic, signaling a given epic event or a given epic character defining the event, must be in the accusative case. When Homer or the rhapsode 'sings' in the accusative that given event or character, he notionally conjures them, bringing them back to life in the process of performance. (It is a common feature of oral poetics that the events mentioned in performance become part of the event that is the performance and that the characters featured in the events become members of the audience attending the performance in the here-and-now.[44]) For example, 535b3–7 features the following "accusatives of the rhapsodic topic" following *âidô* (ᾄδῃς): (1) Odysseus at the epic moment when he leaps upon the threshold, ready to shoot arrows at the suitors; (2) Achilles as he lunges at Hektor; (3) some other highlighted thing

---

[43] Chantraine *DELG* 823.
[44] Cf. in general Martin 1989:xiv, followed by Reynolds 1995:207.

(*ti*, accusative) from epic moments, as when (3a) Andromache bids farewell to Hektor, or from other similar epic moments involving (3b) Hekabe or (3c) Andromache.[45] Compare the Homeric usage of *aeidô* = *âidô* 'narrate' ('sing') + accusative of the topic, such as the anger of Achilles in *Iliad* I 1. Thus the rhapsode's topics are put into the same dimension of heroic-age "reality" as Homer's topics. The rhapsode performs as someone who is parallel to and in continuity with Homer.[46] "Homer," of course, starts his topic at the beginning—as at *Iliad* I 1. As for the rhapsode, his topics can start anywhere in Homer, as we have just seen from the catalogue of heroic topics at *Ion* 535b3–7.

3. *epaineô* + *Homêros* (in accusative) 'quote Homer'. (I continue to use the word "quote" without any implications of textuality.) That is, to "quote" Homer *in medias res*, in a specific context and for a specific purpose: *Ion* 536d6, 541e2 (agent noun *epainetês*, 536d3, 542b4).[47] The specific purposes, as in the *Ion*, have to do with arguing specific points. Compare the usage of *epaineô* in Lycurgus *Against Leokrates* 102, as quoted above, where the orator "quotes" Homer in order to make his specific case. Aside from the various specific purposes involved in this

---

[45] My paraphrase here is meant to match closely Plato's own stylistic *diminuendo* in retelling the contents. All the epic moments that Socrates mentions fall into one of two emotional categories: fear or pity. It is important to stress that Socrates' mention of the performer's weeping (emotion of pity) at 535d3 in front of an audience of 20,000 people [535d4] must refer back to his earlier mention of the rhapsode's performing the sad topic of "piteous things [*eleina*] concerning Andromache," etc. at 535b6ff—just as Socrates' mention of the performer's fright (emotion of fear) at 535d4 must refer back to his earlier mention of the rhapsode's performing frightening topics like that of Odysseus in the action of attacking the suitors or of Achilles in the action of lunging at Hektor. Accordingly, I disagree with Boyd 1994:112, who argues that Socrates' mention of the performer's evocation of pity and fear at 535d1–5 does not refer back to the rhapsode's performing epic scenes of pity and fear at 535b2–7. Boyd wants to argue that the performer described at 535d1–5 is not a rhapsode but an actor in a tragedy. Again, I disagree. See further below.

[46] Extensive discussion in *PP* 60–64.

[47] *BA* 98n on *epaineô* as "the technical word used by *rhapsôidoi* for the notion of 'recite Homer'."

activity of "quoting" Homer, there is of course one overriding general purpose, from an Athenian point of view: that is, the State officially "quotes" Homer to its assembled citizens on the occasion of its highest holiday, the Panathenaia, in the format of rhapsodic competitions. On this occasion, each competing rhapsode gets the chance to "quote" Homer before a general audience of 20,000 persons (535d3)—a round figure that seems notionally equivalent to the body politic of Athens.[48] In this case, to repeat, each competing rhapsode would be required to take up the Homeric narrative continuum where the previous rhapsode had left off. We may compare this rhapsodic imperative with the dramatic imperative of one actor's picking up the dialogue where the previous actor had left off.[49] For the moment, I simply point out that this rhapsodic imperative of maintaining continuum is relevant to the etymology of *epaineô*: 'to continue [*epi-*] making praise [*ainos*] for' (+ accusative of the *laudandus* as the receiver of praise or of the *laudator* as the ultimate giver of praise).[50] By implication, rhapsodic art is a continuation of praise poetry.[51] The idea of continuum is explicit in the *epi-* of *epaineô*.

---

[48] As Mogens Hansen points out to me, the body politic of Athenians is numbered as 20,000 in Demosthenes 25.51. Cf. Murray 1996:122, who adduces Plato *Symposium* 175e6–7, where the size of the audience attending the performances of tragedy at the festival of the Lenaia at Athens in 416 BCE is given as 30,000. On parallelisms between the Panathenaia and the City Dionysia (along with the Lenaia) at Athens as the primary contexts for the evolution of epic and tragic performances, see *PP* 81–82. Correspondingly, Socrates in *Ion* 536a sets up a parallelism between epic *rhapsôidoi* 'rhapsodes' and tragic *hupokritai* 'actors' (*PP* 162).

[49] See also the previous note, concerning parallelisms in the evolution of *rhapsôidoi* 'rhapsodes' and *hupokritai* 'actors'. For more on these parallelisms, see the Appendix.

[50] On the ambiguity of subjective / objective genitives in combination with nouns designating the performance of praise poetry, see *PH* 200n8. The subjective / objective genitives mark respectively the *laudator* and the *laudandus*. This ambiguity seems functional, marking the reciprocity that binds the *laudator* and the *laudandus*.

[51] Note the usage of *epaineô* in the praise poetry of Pindar: *BA* 98, 222–223, 254, 260n; note especially the usage of *epaineô* in Pindar fr. 43 and the commentary in *PH* 424.

4. *dianoia* 'train of thought', applying primarily to *Homer's* train of thought, not to the rhapsode's: 530b10, c3, d3. The rhapsode can enter into this train of thought at any point of the continuum that is the narrative. He can enter into it midstream, *in medias res*. To be able to join the Homeric narrative in progress is to know the *dianoia* of Homer. As such, the rhapsode is the *hermêneus* 'interpreter' of the *dianoia* of Homer (530c3; see no. 5 below). Since the rhapsode can become part of Homer's train of thought, of Homer's *dianoia*, he can also *tell* the thoughts *of* Homer as a verbal commentary (i.e., not necessarily a written commentary) *about* Homer (530c9; see no. 6 below). Such 'commenting' thoughts become, by extension, *dianoiai* as well: 530d3. On Socrates' different 'understanding' of *dianoia*, see no. 6 below. The idea of continuum is explicit in the *dia-* of *dianoia*.

5. *hermêneus* 'interpreter', applied to the rhapsode as one who must know the *dianoia* of Homer on behalf of his audiences: 530c3 (τὸν γὰρ ῥαψῳδὸν ἑρμηνέα δεῖ τοῦ ποιητοῦ τῆς διανοίας γίγνεσθαι τοῖς ἀκούουσι). Here we see the essence of the rhapsode's "hermeneutics": everything depends on his knowing the *dianoia* of Homer (see no. 4).[52] There are further applications of the word *hermêneus* at 535a6, a9 (cf. also 534e4). This concept of an 'interpreter' or 'go-between' acknowledges the reality of a mental gap between Homer on one side and his audience in the here-and-now on the other side. That gap can be bridged by the rhapsode, whose mind can implicitly neutralize the distance that separates the two sides.

6. *legein peri* + *Homêros* (in genitive) 'make a verbal commentary on Homer': 530c9, d2–3. Here Ion is reacting to the claim of Socrates that a rhapsode is expected to be a *hermêneus* 'interpreter' of a poet like Homer, and that therefore Ion must surely know the poet's 'intention', that is, his *dianoia* (531c). By

---

[52] In this sense, the "hermeneutics" of the rhapsode can compensate for the loss of Homer's "original" occasion—and therefore of his "original" meaning. On the poetics of compensation for the lost "original" occasion, cf. *PH* 80n140, with specific reference to the Provençal genre of the *razo*.

using the literary word "intention" here, I am seeking to find a common ground between the specialized Socratic/Platonic understanding of *dianoia* as 'intellect' (e.g. *Republic* VI 511d)[53] and a more general understanding of the word as reflected by the primary definition in the dictionary of LSJ: "thought, i.e. intention, purpose."[54] When Socrates uses the word *dianoia* here at 531c, he understands it to mean Homer's intellectual capacity as revealed by his words (cf. also Aristotle *Poetics* 1450a6, etc.). Affirming his own rhapsodic understanding of *dianoia* as 'train of thought', Ion replies that he can indeed 'speak' most beautifully about Homer, more so than any of his predecessors could speak about Homer (καὶ οἶμαι κάλλιστα ἀνθρώπων λέγειν περὶ Ὁμήρου 530c; cf. 533c–d), and that the *dianoiai* that he 'speaks' about Homer are more beautiful than those spoken by any of his predecessors, including Metrodorus of Lampsacus, Stesimbrotus of Thasos, Glaucon, etc. (ὡς οὔτε Μητρόδωρος ὁ Λαμψακηνὸς οὔτε Στησίμβροτος ὁ Θάσιος οὔτε Γλαύκων οὔτε ἄλλος οὐδεὶς τῶν πώποτε γενομένων ἔσχεν εἰπεῖν οὕτω πολλὰς καὶ καλὰς διανοίας περὶ Ὁμήρου ὅσας ἐγώ 530c–d).[55]

7. *exêgeomai* 'speak authoritatively, make an exegesis' about Homer: 531a7, b8, b9; 533b8; cf. 533b1; at 531a7, the word picks up the idea of *legein peri* + *Homêros* (in genitive) at 530c9.[56] See no. 6 above.

8. *diatribô* 'perform' (that is, perform rhapsodically) at 530b8. Compare Isocrates *Panathenaicus* 19, where **diatribê** refers to the ad hoc performances of 'sophists' at the Lyceum who are described at 18 as 'performing rhapsodically' (*rhapsôidountes*) the poetry of Homer, Hesiod, and other poets; at 33,

---

[53] Cf. Canto 1989:36, 136.

[54] Cf. *PP* 124.

[55] *PP* 124–125. For brief sketches of Metrodorus, Stesimbrotus, and Glaucon, see Murray 1996:103. These names imply the traditions of technical discourse that have shaped the identity of Ion as a rhapsode.

[56] *PP* 125n81.

Isocrates refers again to the same 'sophists' at the Lyceum who are 'performing rhapsodically' (*rhapsôidountas*) and who also 'speak about'—stupidly—Homer, Hesiod, and other poets (*lêreô peri* + genitive; cf. no. 6 above).[57] Their activity of speaking about Homer, Hesiod, and other poets is described as *dialegesthai* (διαλέγοιντο, 18), on which see no. 10 below.

9. *mnêsthênai* (and related forms) 'make mention' concerning a sequence from Homer *within an exegetical frame*, that is, to 'quote' it within such a frame and also to *make comments* or *make a commentary*: e.g. 532c2, 536c7. As in the case of no. 6 above, what is meant is to 'make a verbal commentary'.[58] Where *mnêsthênai* takes the accusative case, it means 'recall', as when Socrates is trying to recall some verses from Homer (ἐὰν μνησθῶ τὰ ἔπη 537a2).[59] The rhapsode notes that his attention is always awakened when someone *mnêsthêi* 'makes commentaries' about Homer (ἐπειδὰν δέ τις περὶ Ὁμήρου μνησθῇ 532c2). Later on in the *Ion*, the same theme of the rhapsode's awakened attention is transferred from the act of making commentaries about the poet (περὶ μὲν Ὁμήρου ὅταν τις μνησθῇ 536c7) to the act of actually performing or 'singing' something from a poet (ἐπειδάν μέν τις ἄλλου του ποιητοῦ ᾄδῃ 536b6).[60] On 'singing', see no. 2 above.

10. *dialegesthai* in the sense of 'engage in dialogue' about a given poet: 532b9 (ὅταν μέν τις περὶ ἄλλου του ποιητοῦ διαλέγηται). It appears in a context that is parallel to that of *mnêsthênai* at 532c.[61] See no. 6 above.

---

[57] *PP* 123–124.

[58] A related form is *mnêmoneuô* 'make verbal commentaries', used in a rhapsodic context by Isocrates *Panathenaicus* 18–19, 33; extensive discussion in *PP* 122–125. The word is not used in Plato's *Ion*.

[59] Cf. *HQ* 152 on the mentality of poetic "total recall" as indicated by the Homeric contrast of *mnê-* + accusative in the sense of 'recall totally' vs. *mnê-* + genitive in the sense of 'make mention of'.

[60] *PP* 125n80.

[61] *PP* 125n80.

Of these ten words, the most pertinent to Plato's own medium is *dialegesthai*. This is the word appropriated by Plato's own medium to designate itself: 'to engage in [Socratic] dialogue' or 'to practice dialectic'. Here we see most clearly that the language of Plato is in direct competition with the language of the rhapsode. Moreover, *dialegesthai* is key to the survival of Socrates' language and of his message.

Plato is fond of exploring the lonely feeling of helplessness on the part of any author who worries about the future life of his written words, which cannot defend themselves if they come under attack (*Phaedrus* 275e, 276c8). One way out is to use the *tekhnê* 'art' that Socrates calls dialectic, *dialektikê* (276e5). The user of this art can plant words into a receptive *psukhê* (e6), and these words will be fertile (277a1) and not sterile (*akarpoi*: a1) like the words planted on a writing surface (276c8). Unlike those written words, these dialectical words can defend not only themselves but also the one who planted them (276e8–277a1), and they can even reproduce themselves into eternity (277a2–3). The words of Socrates must not suffer the fate of written words: Socrates himself could not be saved from death, but his words must be saved, and the antidote to the death of Socratic words is dialectic, that is, Socratic dialogue: as Socrates says in the *Phaedo* (89b9–c1), the only death that he would mourn as a genuine extinction is the death of the *logos*—if it should happen that the *logos* cannot be resurrected (*anabiônai*: 89b10). Socratic *dialegesthai* is vital to the words of Socrates, revitalizing them every time that the reader rereads them. Dialectic is not only the antidote to the death of the words of Socrates: it is also an antidote to the words of the rhapsode.[62] We see a rivalry here in establishing the definitive meaning of *dialegesthai*: rhapsodes

---

[62] In Plato *Phaedrus* 277e I note a revealing reference, made *en passant*, to spoken words that are *rhapsôidoumenoi*, that is, 'performed in the way of rhapsodes'; such words are described as "unexamined and without didactic content" (ἄνευ ἀνακρίσεως καὶ διδαχῆς).

had their own form of *dialegesthai*, as we saw from the indirect testimony of Isocrates (*Panathenaicus* 18), and of Plato himself (*Ion* 532b9).[63] No wonder Plato's Socrates does not allow the rhapsode Ion to have the last word.[64]

The Socratic *dialegesthai* of Plato brings back to life the words of Socrates each time they are read, but it does not bring back Socrates himself. It is not even a certainty, as we see from the *Phaedo*, that *dialegesthai* could ever bring back Socrates' *psukhê*, either. So much for the various Pythagorean scenarios of immortalization for the *psukhê*! Rhapsodic *dialegesthai,* by contrast, brings back to life not only the words of Homer. It brings back Homer himself.

I find it pertinent here to recall a performatively marked saying: "He who laughs last, laughs best."[65] If you ever succeed in saying this saying in just the right context, applying it at just the right moment, you will end up as the definitive speaker of the saying—for the moment. Of course, success will have to depend on your hearers: they have to recognize that you were right after all.

Similarly in the case of Ion as dramatized in Plato's *Ion*: when the rhapsode *epainei* 'quotes' Homer in the context of a debate, applying the poet's *epê* 'words' at a given moment, he expects to win that debate. As we have seen from the *Panathenaicus* of Isocrates, rhapsodes debate by "quoting" Homer. After all, the rhapsode is the definitive speaker of Homer's words; when he speaks them, he even becomes Homer himself.[66] Of course, the rhapsode's success depends on his hearers: he expects them to recognize that he is right in applying the

---

[63] See again above on the rhapsodic concept of *dialegesthai* 'engage in dialogue'.

[64] Cf. Murray 1996:97, who cites Plato *Ion* 530d9 and 536d8 as dramatized instances where Ion would have launched into a commentary if Socrates had not cut him off.

[65] A variation on the "last laugh" topos plays itself out in the joke of "laughing all the way to the bank," as developed in Plato *Ion* 535e4–6.

[66] When the rhapsode says "tell me, Muse," the "me" is notionally Homer: cf. *PP* 61.

words of Homer in any debate because he is the authorized speaker of these words at the authorized occasion for speaking these words. For Athenians in the late fifth century BCE, the dramatic date of Plato's *Ion*, that authorized occasion took place, on a seasonally recurring basis, at the Festival of the Panathenaia.

It was at one such occasion, shortly before the actual event of the rhapsodic competitions took place, that the rhapsode Ion met Socrates. This is the dramatic moment staged by Plato's *Ion*. Of course, Plato will not let Ion win the debate with Socrates. The rhapsode's dialectic must be defeated by the rival dialectic of Socratic dialogue. Not only that: Ion's status as the authorized speaker of Homer's words must be undermined. After all, Socrates too can perform Homeric poetry, and he can even out-argue the rhapsode on the basis of that poetry. Are we to conclude, then, that Socrates can replace Ion as the medium or mediator of Homer? Are the rhapsodes no longer indispensable for the mediation of Homer?

The answer, from the historical standpoint of the late fifth century BCE and even thereafter, is simple: Socrates cannot replace Ion. Nor will he ever replace him—so long as there exists a Panathenaic Festival featuring as one of its main events the performance of Homer by rhapsodes. In saying "there exists a Panathenaic Festival," I am using the present tense to symbolize the synchronic dimension of my formulation, anchored for the moment in the historical period of the late fifth century. From a synchronic point of view, there is one thing Ion does that Socrates can never do and can never take away from Ion: Socrates can never replace Ion as an authorized performer of Homeric poetry at the Panathenaia.

Such a point of view, of course, would be a traditional one. From a more modernizing point of view, however, Socrates seems to have the last laugh on the rhapsode. Why care about performances of Homeric poetry at the Panathenaia or anywhere else? Since we have Homer in books, who needs rhapsodes in the first place? Who would possibly need Ion now? Plato's Socrates can read Homer for us better than Ion can. For that matter, we do not need Socrates, either, once he has liberated us from the rhapsodes: now we can read Homer on our own. Homer is there for us as a text, recorded in books, ready for us to interpret, ready for our own modern commentaries. There is no need for the rhapsode as an exegete, as a *hermêneus*. And we certainly do not need the rhapsode's performance. We now have Homer in writing—or maybe we have always had Homer in writing. And surely the text of Homer is more reliable than any performance of Homer. Even the transmission of the text is surely more reliable than the transmission of the performance. Even if there is some risk that the transmission of the written texts may become corrupted, there is surely a greater risk of interference in the transmission of performance. In Plato's *Ion*, the rhapsode of "today" is visualized as the last and weakest link in a long magnetic chain of successive generations of performers connected all the way back to the original magnet, Homer (533d–536d). Thanks to the text of Homer, we can now cut out that whole succession of intermediate performers. Thanks to the text, we now have direct access to Homer.

What is missing in this picture? I suggest that a diachronic perspective is needed. From such a perspective, the art of Ion actually derives from that succession of previous rhapsodes. Even the Homeric tradition derives from that succession. From a diachronic point of view, the rhapsodes' derivation from "Homer" is itself an ongoing process of creation and re-creation. We have to take seriously the historical fact that Ion, as a rhapsode, was an authorized performer of Homer, and that the authorization of rhapsodic performances came from the authority of the Athenian State, on the authoritative occasion of the Panathenaia.[67] If we took the Panathenaia seriously as the most authoritative context for studying the transmission of the Homeric tradition, instead of Plato's reading of the Homeric text, then Ion might after all have the last laugh.

---

[67] I note, with special interest, the golden garland that Ion expects to win at the Panathenaia, to be awarded by the Homeridai (Plato *Ion* 530d). The political authority of the state seems to be linked with the poetic authority of the Homeridai.

Chapter 2
Epic as Music:
Rhapsodic Models of Homer in Plato's
Timaeus and Critias[1]

Plato's *Timaeus* and *Critias* contain valuable references
to the performative techniques of *rhapsôidoi* or 'rhapsodes' and
to the compositional techniques of Homeric poetry. These techniques belong to the *tekhnê* 'art' known to Plato and his contem-
poraries as *mousikê*.[2] The word's meaning is self-evident:
mousikê is the art of the Muses. As we will see from the testimony of inscriptions and other evidence, this term *mousikê*
included the 'music' of (1) rhapsodes, (2) citharodes = cithara-
singers = singers self-accompanied by the cithara or 'lyre', (3)
aulodes = aulos-singers = singers accompanied by the aulos or
'pipe', (4) cithara-players, and (5) aulos-players. In Plato's time,
the high point of this kind of *mousikê* in the civic calendar of
Athens was the Festival of the Panathenaia.[3] Primarily by way of

---

[1] The original version of this essay is N 2000a.

[2] See especially Plato *Laws* VI 764c–765d, to be discussed below.

[3] For Plato, the term *mousikê* also included the "music" of *khorôidia*, the singing and
dancing of a *khoros* 'chorus': see Plato *Laws* 764e (in this passage, *khorôidia* is explicitly connected with *orkhêsis* 'dancing' as well as singing). By default, Plato (ibid.) designates as *monôidia* all forms of *mousikê* that are not *khorôidia* (such a designation is
problematic, because *monôidia* does not account for the "music" of such categories as
solo cithara-playing and solo aulos-playing). A primary form of *khorôidia* was the
choral ode of tragedy and comedy. In Plato's time and earlier, the high point of this
kind of *mousikê* in the civic calendar of Athens was the Festival of the Dionysia (also,
secondarily, the Festival of the Lenaia). From the standpoint of the Classical period of
the fifth century, tragedy and comedy *per se* are not "music." For Plato, *mousikê*
applies to *khorôidia* only, which is just one aspect of tragedy and comedy. In the
Classical period, the "music" of tragedy and comedy *per se* is not officially inspired
by the Muses: hence it is not technically *mousikê*, which is the "art" or *tekhnê* of the
Muses. In later periods, however, such distinctions are blurred by the growing profes-
sionalization of theatrical performances, as we see from the evolution of such institutions as the *Dionusou tekhnitai* in the early third century (cf. *PP* 174n74 and 177n89).

the *Timaeus* and the *Critias* of Plato, in addition to his definitive work concerning rhapsodes, the *Ion*, we can make considerable progress in reconstructing a central event in the *agônes* or 'contests' of *mousikê* at the Panathenaic Festival of Athens, that is, rhapsodic competitions in the performance of Homer. Also, the *Timaeus* and the *Critias* reveal details about the "musical" techniques of rhapsodes and of "Homer" himself. These details provide a basis for understanding the nature of the *Timaeus* and the *Critias* as artistic—even "rhapsodic"—productions in their own right.

It is important to start by stressing that the rhapsodic performances of Homer at the Panathenaic Festival were based on the principle of *competition*. The key word is *agôn* 'competition, contest, ordeal', as evoked in the striking expression of Friedrich Nietzsche, "der agonale Geist."[4] The agonistic principle underlying the rhapsodic performances of Homer at the Panathenaia is evident in Plato's *Ion*. This dialogue is named after a rhapsode from Ephesus who comes to Athens to compete for first prize at the Panathenaia (καὶ τὰ Παναθήναια νικήσομεν, *Ion* 530b2). Plato's wording makes it explicit that the occasion for the performing of Homer by rhapsodes at the Panathenaia is in effect a *competition* or *contest* among rhapsodes, an *agôn* (ἀγῶνα at *Ion* 530a5, picked up by ἠγωνίζου and ἠγωνίσω at a8), and that the agonistic art of the *rhapsôidoi* 'rhapsodes' falls under the general category of *mousikê* (μουσικῆς at a7). These words *agôn* and *mousikê* are essential for understanding the traditional art or *tekhnê* of the rhapsodes.[5]

---

[4] Cf. Berve 1966.

[5] The principle of *agôn* is common to the "music" of epic and the "music" of tragedy / comedy. Like the Festival of the Panathenaia, the Festivals of the Dionysia and the Lenaia were a setting for *agôn* 'competition' among composers of what we would call "music": see especially Plato *Laws* VIII 835a. See also *PH* 386–387 and 401–403, especially with reference to Euripides *Bacchae* 975 and Aristophanes *Wasps* 1439. Still, tragedy and comedy are not *mousikê*: only the *khorôidia* of tragedy and comedy is *mousikê*. See above.

Let us start with *mousikê,* as mentioned in the passage just cited, Plato *Ion* 530a7. To repeat, the word's meaning should be self-evident: *mousikê* is the art or *tekhnê* of the Muses. And yet, as we shall see, *mousikê* is subject to misunderstandings. Accordingly, it is essential to stress right away what our passage in Plato *Ion* 530a7 indicates clearly: that the art of *mousikê* includes the art of the rhapsode.[6] The art or *tekhnê* of *mousikê* is an agonistic art: those who practice this *tekhnê* must compete with each other in formal and institutionalized competitions called *agônes.*

At the Panathenaia, there are *agônes* of *mousikê* not only for rhapsodes but also for *kitharôidoi* 'citharodes' [= cithara-singers], *aulôidoi* 'aulodes' [= aulos-singers], cithara-players, and aulos-players, as we learn directly from an Athenian inscription dated at around 380 BCE, IG II^2 2311, which records the winners of Panathenaic prizes.[7] We also learn about these categories of "musical" competition from Plato *Laws* VI 764d–e (mention of rhapsodes, cithara-singers, and aulos-players), where the wording makes it clear that the point of reference is the Panathenaia.[8] The wording also makes it clear that competition is involved: this kind of *mousikê* is described as 'agonistic', *agônistikê* (*Laws* VI 764d). In fact, the only aspect of *mousikê* that is not overtly competitive is the educational: *mousikê* is subdivided into two aspects, *agônistikê* and *paideia* (*Laws* VI 764c6–7).

As we take a closer look at the Panathenaic inscription dated at around 380 BCE, we may notice straight off that the winning competitors received prizes of high monetary value: for example, the first prize in the competitions of citharodes was a

---

[6] Conversely, to repeat, the art of *mousikê* does not technically include the overall art of the dramatist of tragedy or comedy.

[7] For an introduction to this inscription, see Parke 1977:35.

[8] In Plato *Laws* VI 764e and VIII 835a, the officials in charge of these *agônes* 'competitions' in *mousikê* are specified as *athlothetai.* As we will see from what follows, these officials are specific to the Panathenaia.

crown of gold worth 1000 drachmas in addition to 500 silver drachmas. This same inscription must have mentioned the prize-winning rhapsodes at the beginning of the document, lines 1–3, where the stone is broken off. It is unfortunate that the break happens at exactly the point where we would expect the victorious rhapsodes to be listed.[9] The author of a most influential work on the Panathenaia, J.A. Davison, has expressed doubt that this fourth-century BCE inscription had mentioned the prize-winning rhapsodes at lines 1–3,[10] adding: "rhapsodic competitions are known only to the literary tradition."[11]

But there is in fact a very important piece of direct epigraphical evidence about rhapsodic competitions. The document in question comes from a city other than Athens. It is IG XII ix 189, an inscription from the city of Eretria in Euboea (ca. 341/0 BCE) concerning a festival of Artemis.[12] Right at the beginning, the program of the Artemisia is explicitly formulated:[13]

τιθεῖν τὴμ πόλιν ἀγῶνα μουσικῆς

that the city is to organize a competition [agôn] of mousikê.

IG XII ix 189.5

As we read on, we find more details:

τὴν δὲ μουσικὴν τιθεῖν ῥαψωιδοῖς,| αὐλωιδοῖς, κιθαρισταῖς, κιθαρωιδοῖς, παρωιδοῖς,| τοὺς δὲ τὴν

---

[9] Parke 1977:35.

[10] Davison 1968:56. The IG II[2] 2311 edition conjectures "citharists" rather than "rhapsodes" for the lacuna.

[11] Davison 1968:56n2.

[12] PP 111n24. For more on this inscription, see Nilsson 1906:239.

[13] I alert the reader, in advance, to the "culture shock" of the Euboean dialect (e.g. shortening of η to ει, rhotacism of sigma, etc.).

μουσικὴν ἀγωνιζομένους πάντα[ς] | ἀγωνίζεσθαι
προσόδιον τεῖ θυσίει ἐν τεῖ αὐλεῖ ἔ[χο]ντας τὴν
σκευὴν ἥμπερ ἐν τοῖ ἀγῶνι ἔχουρ[ι]

… and that [the city] is to organize the *mousikê* for rhapsodes, aulodes [= aulos-singers], cithara-players, citharodes [cithara-singers], and parody-singers; further, that
those who compete [*agônizomai*] in the *mousikê* should
all compete [*agônizomai*] in the *prosodion* [= processional song] for the sacrifice [*thusia*][14] in the *aulê*, having the same costume that they have in the competition
proper.

IG XII ix 189.10–15

This inscription from Eretria contains valuable comparative evidence for helping us understand the *agônes* of *mousikê* at
the Panathenaia in Athens. These Athenian competitions seem to
be the historical basis for the theoretical models discussed in
Plato *Laws* VI 764d–e, where we read of competition (*agônistikê*
d5) in *mousikê* (d6) for rhapsodes, citharodes, auletes [= pipe-
players], and so on (other categories are not specified).[15] Such
theoretical references in the *Laws*, I argue, are based on the specific historical realities of the Panathenaia.

Moving beyond Plato, we may turn to Aristotle for a less
theoretical and more historical perspective on the Panathenaia.
Aristotle gives a brief outline of the main features of the
Panathenaia at Athens in his *Constitution of the Athenians*
60.1–3:

1. *agôn* 'competition' in *mousikê* (τὸν ἀγῶνα τῆς
μουσικῆς); prizes awarded: gold and silver.

---

[14] More on the implications of the *thusia* 'sacrifice' in the discussion below.

[15] Extended discussion of the parallelisms linking rhapsodes, citharodes, aulodes:
PH 54, 85–104.

2. *agôn* 'competition' in athletics (τὸν γυμνικὸν ἀγῶνα), including equestrian events (horse-racing and chariot-racing: ἱπποδρομίαν); prizes awarded: Panathenaic amphoras containing olive oil.

3. *peplos* 'robe' = the ceremonial robe, Peplos (τὸν πέπλον); woven for the goddess Athena, it was formally presented to her at the Panathenaia.

4. *pompê* 'procession' = the Panathenaic Procession (τήν τε πομπὴν τῶν Παναθηναίων); at the climax of this procession, the Peplos was formally presented to Athena. Aristotle does not say it explicitly, but the occasion of this climactic moment is a *thusia* 'sacrifice', more on which later.

5. *athlothetai* = a board of ten magistrates, with one from each *phulê* appointed (by lot) every four years for a term of four years; their function was to organize and supervise all the events of no. 1, no. 2, no. 3, and no. 4, including the arranging and awarding of prizes in the case of no. 1 and no. 2.

For the moment, I have kept this outline at a minimum, recapping as closely as possible the main features as reported by Aristotle (he orders them differently, however: 5, 4, 1, 2, 3).

Aristotle's reference in *Constitution of the Athenians* 60.1 to an *agôn* 'competition' in *mousikê* (τὸν ἀγῶνα τῆς μουσικῆς) which he says was held at the Panathenaia does not make explicit the correlation of rhapsodic competitions with the citharodic, the aulodic, and so on. Aristotle's elliptic reference has led to some confusion about the "musical contests" of the Panathenaia, and the conventional but anachronistic translation "musical" confuses the matter even further, since the English word seems to suggest, misleadingly, an exclusion of *rhapsôidoi* 'rhapsodes' and the inclusion only of *kitharôidoi* 'citharodes',

41

aulôidoi 'aulodes', and so on.[16] Still, what I infer to be implicit in Aristotle's statement is made explicit in a corresponding mention of the Panathenaia by Isocrates, *Panegyricus* 159, whose words specify that *Homeric* performances were taking place 'in *athla* [contests] of *mousikê*', ἐν τοῖς μουσικοῖς ἄθλοις.[17] Other sources too provide explicit evidence about the institution of rhapsodic contests at the Panathenaia, and many of these specify the correlation of contests in athletics with contests in *mousikê*.[18]

The rhapsodes at the Panathenaia not only competed with each other in performing the poetry of Homer: they also had to take turns following the narrative sequence of that poetry in the process of competition. In the *Hipparkhos* of "pseudo-Plato," as we have seen in the previous chapter, there is a story that purports to explain an Athenian law requiring that the *Iliad* and *Odyssey* be performed *in sequence* by the *rhapsôidoi* 'rhapsodes' at the Panathenaia:

[16] The term "musical" is used by Davison 1968:56. As we have seen, Davison even expresses doubt that the 4th-century BCE inscription of Panathenaic prizes, IG II[2] 2311, had mentioned the prize-winning rhapsodes at the beginning of the list, where the inscription is broken off. In his commentary on Aristotle *Constitution of the Athenians* 60.1, Rhodes 1981:670–671 does not mention rhapsodic contests, speaking only generally of "musical contests." For evidence in the visual arts on rhapsodic competitions at the Panathenaia, see Shapiro 1993, who disputes some commonly-held assumptions about representations of competing rhapsodes (for example, he argues convincingly that the performer represented on Side A of the red-figure neck amphora [London, British Museum E270], ca. 500–490 BCE, is an aulode, not a rhapsode).

[17] See *PP* 111n24.

[18] There is a collection of testimonia assembled by Kotsidu 1991:243–292. In Plato *Laws* VIII 828b–c, we see a collocation of the noun *agônes* with the adjectives *mousikoi* and *gumnikoi*, mentioned in the context of *athlothetai*. The latter term makes clear a Panathenaic context, as we know from Aristotle's reference to these officials, mentioned above. Cf. Plato *Laws* VIII 834e–835a: again *mousikê*, again specifically including rhapsodes, mentioned again in the context of *athlothetai*. Cf. also Plato *Laws* VI 764d–e: *agôn* of *mousikê*, specifically including rhapsodes as well as citharodes, etc.

Ἱππάρχῳ ... ὃς ἄλλα τε πολλὰ καὶ καλὰ ἔργα
σοφίας ἀπεδείξατο, καὶ τὰ Ὁμήρου ἔπη πρῶτος
ἐκόμισεν εἰς τὴν γῆν ταυτηνί, καὶ ἠνάγκασε τοὺς
ῥαψῳδοὺς Παναθηναίοις ἐξ ὑπολήψεως ἐφεξῆς
αὐτὰ διιέναι, ὥσπερ νῦν ἔτι οἵδε ποιοῦσιν

Hipparkhos, ... who made a public demonstration of
many and beautiful accomplishments to manifest his
expertise [*sophia*], especially by being the first to bring
over [*komizô*] to this land [= Athens] the poetic utterances [*epê*] of Homer, and he forced the rhapsodes [*rhapsôidoi*] at the Panathenaia to go through [*diienai*] these
utterances in sequence [*ephexês*], by relay [*hupolêpsis*],
just as they [= the rhapsodes] do even nowadays.

"Plato" *Hipparkhos* 228b–c

In this extract, I have highlighted two words with special
rhapsodic implications: *ephexês* 'in sequence' and *hupolêpsis*,
which I translate as 'relay' for reasons that I have already out-
lined in the previous chapter. In the present chapter, I concentrate
on the expression *ephexês auta diienai* 'go through them [= the
epê 'poetic utterances' of Homer] in sequence', to which I will
compare the contexts of Plato *Timaeus* 23d3–4 / 24a1–2: *panta
... hexês dielthein / ephexês diienai* 'go through everything in
sequence' / 'go through in sequence'. At a later point in the present chapter, we will return to these contexts in the *Timaeus*.

As in the previous chapter, I supplement the passage just
quoted from the *Hipparkhos* with a passage taken from a speech
delivered by the Athenian statesman Lycurgus (330 BCE):

βούλομαι δ' ὑμῖν καὶ τὸν Ὅμηρον παρασχέσθαι
ἐπαινῶν. οὕτω γὰρ ὑπέλαβον ὑμῶν οἱ πατέρες
σπουδαῖον εἶναι ποιητήν, ὥστε νόμον ἔθεντο καθ'
ἑκάστην πενταετηρίδα τῶν Παναθηναίων μόνου

τῶν ἄλλων ποιητῶν ῥαψῳδεῖσθαι τὰ ἔπη, ἐπίδειξιν ποιούμενοι πρὸς τοὺς Ἕλληνας ὅτι τὰ κάλλιστα τῶν ἔργων προῃροῦντο.

I wish to adduce[19] for you Homer, quoting [*epaineô*]
him,[20] since the reception[21] that he had from your ancestors made him so important a poet that there was a law
enacted by them that requires, every fourth year of the
Panathenaia, the rhapsodic performing [*rhapsôideô*] of
his poetic utterances [*epê*]—his alone and no other
poet's. In this way they [= your ancestors] made a
demonstration [*epideixis*],[22] intended for all Hellenes to
see, that they made a conscious choice of the most noble
of accomplishments.

Lycurgus *Against Leokrates* 102

As I noted in the previous chapter, I infer from these two
passages that the Homeric *epê* 'poetic utterances' performed at
the Panathenaia were the *Iliad* and *Odyssey*. According to these
passages, there existed in Athens a custom of maintaining a fixed
narrative sequence of Homeric performance at the Panathenaia.
According to this custom, known to classicists as the
"Panathenaic Rule," each performing rhapsode was required to
take up the narration where the previous rhapsode left off.

---

[19] I stress my observation in the previous chapter: the orator, by "adducing" the classical authors (I mean "classical" from his synchronic point of view), assumes the role
of statesman.

[20] For *epaineô* in the sense of 'quote', see the discussion in the previous chapter.

[21] In rhapsodic terminology, as we saw above in "Plato" *Hipparkhos* 228b–c, *hupolêpsis* is not just 'reception' but also 'continuation' in the sense of reception by way of
relay.

[22] Cf. the context of *epideigma* 'display, demonstration' in "Plato" *Hipparkhos* 228d,
as discussed in *PH* 161; cf. also *PH* 217 and following on *apodeixis* 'presentation,
demonstration'. The basic idea behind what is being "demonstrated" is a *model for
performance*.

As we saw earlier, the Panathenaic event of Homeric performances by rhapsodes is designated by ancient sources in terms of an *agôn* or an *athlon*, both words meaning 'competition' or 'contest'. Thus there are really two aspects of the Panathenaic Rule: not only must the rhapsodes take turns as they perform the *Iliad* and *Odyssey* in sequence, they must also compete with each other in the process.[23]

These two aspects of the Panathenaic Rule, sequencing *and* competition, are neatly reflected in two different mythologized versions of the concept of the rhapsode, as reported in the scholia to Pindar *Nemean* 2.1:

οἱ δέ φασι τῆς Ὁμήρου ποιήσεως μὴ ὑφ᾿ ἓν συν-
ηγμένης, σποράδην δὲ ἄλλως καὶ κατὰ μέρη
διῃρημένης, ὁπότε ῥαψῳδοῖεν αὐτήν, εἱρμῷ τινι
καὶ ῥαφῇ παραπλήσιον ποιεῖν, εἰς ἓν αὐτὴν
ἄγοντας

And some say that—since the poetry of Homer had been in a state of not being brought together <u>under the heading of one thing</u>,[24] but instead, in a negative sense [= ἄλλως], had been in the state of being scattered and divided into parts—whenever they would <u>perform</u> it <u>rhapsodically</u> they would be doing something that is similar to <u>sequencing</u> or <u>sewing</u>, as they brought it together <u>into one thing</u>.

[version 1 at 2.1c]

---

[23] I confront for the first time this competitive aspect of rhapsodic performance in *PH* 23–24n28.

[24] My translation here is attempting to capture the metaphorical implications of *hupo* in the sense of 'under'.

οἱ δέ, ὅτι κατὰ μέρος πρότερον τῆς ποιήσεως διαδεδομένης τῶν ἀγωνιστῶν ἕκαστος ὅ τι βούλοιτο μέρος ᾖδε, τοῦ δὲ ἄθλου τοῖς νικῶσιν ἀρνὸς ἀποδεδειγμένου προσαγορευθῆναι τότε μὲν ἀρνῳδούς, αὖθις δὲ ἑκατέρας τῆς ποιήσεως εἰσενεχθείσης τοὺς ἀγωνιστὰς οἷον ἀκουμένους πρὸς ἄλληλα τὰ μέρη καὶ τὴν σύμπασαν ποίησιν ἐπιόντας, ῥαψῳδοὺς προσαγορευθῆναι, ταῦτά φησι Διονύσιος ὁ Ἀργεῖος

Others say that previously — since the poetry had been divided into parts, with each of the competitors [agônistai] singing whichever part he wanted, and since the designated prize for the winners had been a lamb — [those competitors] were in those days called arnôidoi [= lamb-singers], but then, later on — since the competitors [agônistai], whenever each of the two poems was introduced, were mending the parts to each other, as it were, and moving toward the whole poem—they were called rhapsôidoi. These things are said by Dionysius of Argos [between fourth and third centuries BCE; FGH 308 F 2]

[version 2 at 2.1d]

The myth in version 2, which restates the principle of sequencing as stated in the myth of version 1, adds the principle of competition. According to version 2, the principle of competition was there all along, and the principle of sequencing was added to it only later. So we have here a myth that narrates an "evolution" of sorts, from an unsequenced competition for the prize of an arên 'lamb' to a sequenced competition for a prize that is no longer that of a lamb.[25] The rhapsodes no longer compete for the prize of a lamb, *but they still compete with each other even as they "sew together" the parts of the two poems.* The two aspects of the Panathenaic Rule are hereby both aetiologized. That the myth refers to the Panathenaic Rule is indicated by the explicit reference to two poems: when we combine this detail with the testimony of Lycurgus, we can see that the Rule applies to the *Iliad* and the *Odyssey*.

The myth in version 2 motivates the principle of rhapsodic competition in terms of the institution of sacrifice, specifically the sacrifice of an *arên* 'lamb'. In this connection, let us return to the inscription from Eretria that we have just considered, concerning *agônes* 'competitions' of *mousikê*. We find here a remarkable analogy with the myth in version 2, since these Eretrian competitions of *mousikê* are motivated, again, in terms of the institution of sacrifice, specifically the sacrifice of *arnes* 'lambs'. In this case, however, the motivation is formulated explicitly from the synchronic viewpoint of the organizers of the festival themselves. At the very beginning of the Eretrian inscription we read:

[θ]εο[ί].Ι Ἐξήκεστος Διοδώρου εἶπεν· ὅπωρ ἄν τὰ Ἀρͱτεμίρια ὡς κάλλιστα ἄγωμεν καὶ θύω[ριν ὡς πͿλεͿῖστοι, ἔδοξεν τεῖ βουλεῖ καὶ τοῖ δήμοιΙ[ ] τιθεῖν τὴμ πόλιν ἀγῶνα μουσικῆς ἀπὸ χιλίων Ι δραχμῶν τεῖ Μεταξὺ καὶ τεῖ Φυλακεῖ καὶ παρέχειͿν ἄρνας τεῖ πρὸ τῶν Ἀρτεμιρίων πέντε ἡμέρας, τΙούτων δὲ δύο ἐγκρίτους εἶναι

(Invocation to the gods.) Exekestos son of Diodoros spoke: in order that the Artemisia [= Festival of Artemis] be conducted by us in the most beautiful way possible and <u>in order that as many people as possible may make sacrifice</u> [= *thuô*], it was decided by the Boule and the

---

[25] In light of e.g. *Iliad* III 103, we may retranslate *arên* as 'sheep' (of either sex) instead of 'lamb'.

Demos that the city is to organize a competition [*agôn*] of *mousikê*, at the expense of 1000 drachmas, on the days Metaxu and Phulakê,[26] and that (the city) is to provide lambs [= *arnes*] on the day that is five days before the Artemisia, and, of these [lambs], two are to be *enkritoi* [specially selected (for sacrifice)].[27]

IG XII ix 189.1–8

The inscription goes on to specify that the *mousikê* should begin on the fourth day before the end of the month of Anthesterion (lines 8–10: ἄρχειν δὲ τῆς μο|υσικῆς τετράδα φθίνοντος τοῦ ᾿Ανθεστηρι|ῶνος μηνός). Then the inscription lists the categories of competition in *mousikê* (lines 10–14), and I repeat here my translation of the wording: "and that [the city] is to organize the *mousikê* for rhapsodes, aulodes, citharists, citharodes, and parody-singers; further, that those who compete [*agônizomai*] in the *mousikê* should all compete [*agônizomai*] in the *prosodion* [= processional song] for the sacrifice [*thusia*] in the *aulê*, having the same costume that they have in the competition proper." As at the beginning of the inscription, we see here again the highlighting of *thusia* 'sacrifice' (line 13) as the central theme of the institution of competitions in *mousikê*.

The climactic sacrifice at the place called the *aulê* is marked by a *prosodion* 'processional song' (line 13) in which all the competitors in the individual competitions of *mousikê* are to "compete" in a preliminary way. I infer that this merged "competition" is a sort of preview of the individual competitions, after which the *athla* 'competitive prizes' (line 15) are to be awarded (lines 15–20):[28]

---

[26] My interpretation here is not certain.

[27] On the semantics of *enkrisis* in the sense of a "choice selection" in a competitive context, see LSJ pp. 473–474.

[28] I infer that these prize-allotments correspond to the actual winners on the first occasion of the institution as prescribed by the inscription; on this occasion, I infer further, no aulodes entered the competitions in *mousikê*.

48

category	prizes	drachmas
rhapsodes	1st prize:	120
	2nd:	30
	3rd:	20
aulodes (boys' category)	1st:	50
	2nd:	30
citharists	1st:	110
	2nd:	70
	3rd:	55
citharodes	1st:	200
	2nd:	150
	3rd:	100
parody-singers	1st:	50
	2nd:	10

The inscription goes on to specify the details of per diem payments to be made to the *agônistai* 'contestants' (line 20): one drachma daily, starting no more than three days before what is called the *pro-agôn* at line 22 and extending up to the point where the *agôn* proper takes place (μέ|χρι οὗ ἂν ὁ ἀγὼν γένηται, lines 22–23).[29]

In reality, then, the contestants compete for cash prizes. Notionally, however, the prizes are sacrificial, in that they are awarded in the context of a grand *thusia* 'sacrifice' inaugurated by a *prosodion* 'processional song' in which all the contestants notionally "compete" in a preliminary *agôn*, that is, in the *pro-*

---

[29] In this context (line 23), it is not clear to me whether *agôn* 'competition' refers to the individual contestant's occasion for competing or to the competition in *mousikê* writ large. The first alternative raises interesting questions: are there different days of *agôn* for different contestants? (The day of the *pro-agôn* must be the same for all.)

agôn mentioned at line 22. Moreover, this processional song is the climax of an actual procession, *pompê* (line 39), in which all the *agônistai* 'competitors' of the *mousikê* are required to participate (lines 37–38). The explicit reason given for this required participation of competitors is this:

ὅπως ἂν ὡς καλλίσστη ἡ πομπὴ καὶ ἡ θυσίη γένηται

in order that the procession [*pompê*] and the sacrifice [*thusia*] become the most beautiful possible[30]

IG XII ix 189.39

The homology between the *pompê* 'procession' and the *thusia* 'sacrifice' is highlighted by the syntax (ἡ πομπὴ καὶ ἡ θυσίη, line 39). The competitors in *mousikê*, then, participate in and become part of the entire religious program of the Artemisia, a continuum that extends from the procession to the climactic sacrifice and from the sacrifice to the competitions themselves.

This homology between procession and sacrifice—not even to mention the religious mentality of sequencing that connects one to the other—is strikingly parallel to what we find at the Panathenaia in Athens. On that seasonally-recurring occasion as well, though of course on a vastly larger scale, we see a procession climaxing in a sacrifice: the Panathenaic Procession starts from the Kerameikos and passes through the Agora and ends up on the heights of the Acropolis, reaching its climax in a grand sacrifice within the sacred space of Athena on high. The Parthenon Frieze gives a mythologically synchronic picture of

---

[30] A dominant theme in this inscription is the idea conveyed by *kallist-* 'most beautiful': see also lines 1–3 as quoted above: "in order that the Artemisia [= Festival of Artemis] be conducted by us in the most beautiful way possible [*kallista*] and in order that as many people as possible may make sacrifice [= *thuô*]." Perhaps we may connect this theme with the cult-epithet of Artemis, *kallistê* 'most beautiful'.

the whole *continuum* of the Panathenaic Procession as it approaches its climax in the sacrifice to Athena.[31]

From the evidence of such comparisons between the Artemisia of Eretria and the Panathenaia of Athens, I infer that we are dealing here with two institutions that are not only parallel but even cognate. A particularly telling point of comparison, as I have stressed, is the custom of holding *agônes* 'competitions' in *mousikê*. The categories of competition are remarkably parallel, even in the relative rankings of these categories.

There is, granted, a vast difference in scale between the Artemisia of Eretria, as recorded in the inscription IG XII ix 189 from ca. 341/0 BCE, and the Panathenaia of Athens, as recorded in the inscription IG II^2 2311 from 380 BCE. That year at the Panathenaia, as I have already noted, the monetary value of the first prize in the competition of citharodes, a gold crown, was worth 1000 drachmas—and that figure does not even include the additional cash prize of silver worth 500 drachmas. When we compare that sum of 1000 drachmas at the Panathenaia of that time to the sum of 200 drachmas, which was the cash prize for first place in the competition of citharodes at the Artemisia of Eretria just forty-odd years later, we can appreciate all the more the magnitude of the Panathenaia. The monetary value of the gold crown bestowed on the top citharode at the Panathenaia of 380 BCE is the equivalent of the entire budget of the Artemisia in 341/0 BCE.

Despite the differences in scale, the Eretrian inscription IG XII ix 189 shows enough structural parallelisms with the Panathenaia to encourage extrapolations in areas where we do not have direct information about the Athenian festival. Here I return to the all-important elements of procession and sacrifice. The districts of the city, called *khôroi*, are each to contribute animals (cattle are specified) that are *krita* 'chosen' by state

---

[31] Cf. B. Nagy 1992, who also argues that the *athlothetai* are actually represented on the Frieze.

overseers for the sacrifice (lines 25–31). Sacrificial animals can also be bought, in the sacred precinct, by individual sacrificers from individual sellers (31–34), as also in the agora (35). All those who wish to sacrifice are to march in the procession, which is to be marshaled in the agora by officials called *dêmarkhoi* (34–35); the sacrificial animals are to be led in the procession by their respective sacrificers, in a prescribed sequence determined by the categories of animals: first come the *dêmosia* or victims of the State, including the choicest entry or *kallisteion* 'fairest prize' (35–36); then come the *krita* 'chosen ones', presumably the ones contributed by the *khôroi* (36); and then, finally, all other victims, elliptically indicated by a formula that refers not to the animals but to their sacrificers, and this category includes any private individual who wishes to participate in the procession (*sumpompeuein*: 37).

It is essential to stress here a detail just noted, that the organizers of the procession culminating in the grand sacrifice are officials called the *dêmarkhoi* (34–35). Earlier on in the inscription, these same *dêmarkhoi* are described as the officials in charge of the entire *agôn* of *mousikê* (τὸν δὲ ἀγῶνα τιθόντων οἱ δήμιαρχοι, 23–24). By extrapolation, we can say that the *dêmarkhoi* of the Artemisia are analogous to the *athlothetai* of the Panathenaia.

Participation in the grand procession of the Artemisia, then, is an option open to any individual. For the actual competitors in the *mousikê*, however, participation is required. The inscription specifies that all the *agônistai* 'competitors' are to take part in the procession (37–38), and we have already noted the explicit reason given for this required participation: " in order that the procession [*pompê*] and the sacrifice [*thusia*] become the most beautiful possible " (39). Since the other participants in the procession are conducting the various sacrificial animals to the grand sacrifice, can we say the same for the competitors as well? If so, perhaps the sacrificial animals to be conducted by the competitors are the lambs mentioned at the beginning of the inscription, the *enkritoi* of line 8.

The inscription ends by providing for its words to be inscribed on a stele and to be placed in the precinct of Artemis (40–41), with the following express purpose:

ὅπως ἂν κατὰ τοῦτα γίλνηται ἡ θυσίη καὶ ἡ μουσικὴ τεῖ Ἀρτέμιδι εἰς τὸν ἀεὶ χ|[ρό]νον

so that, according to these specifications, the *thusia* 'sacrifice' and the *mousikê* for Artemis may last forever

IG XII ix 189.41–42

One last time we see the all-important factor of sacrifice, and, this time, the homology is between the *thusia* 'sacrifice' and the *mousikê*.

A parallel homology is at work in the *Timaeus* of Plato. The dramatized occasion of this dialogue is "the *thusia* of the goddess" (τῇ ... τῆς θεοῦ θυσίᾳ 26e3), that is, the Panathenaia.[32] The story of Atlantis and Athens, about to be narrated by Critias, is described by him metaphorically as a *humnos* to be sung as an encomium of the goddess: to recall the story, he says, would be a fitting way both to please Socrates "and at the same time to praise the goddess on the occasion of her Festival in a righteous and truthful way, just as if we were making her the subject of a *humnos* " (καὶ τὴν θεὸν ἅμα ἐν τῇ πανηγύρει δικαίως τε καὶ ἀληθῶς οἷόνπερ ὑμνοῦντας ἐγκωμιάζειν 21a2–3).[33]

---

[32] Brisson 1982:38.

[33] Precisely in this context, *Timaeus* 20e, Plato evokes the first sentence of Herodotus, the so-called prooemium of the *History*: see *PH* 226. For the performance of epic, the *humnos* as a genre is the equivalent of a prooemium, as we see from the reference in Thucydides (3.104.3–4) to the *Homeric Hymn to Apollo* as a *prooimion* 'prooemium'. Cf. *PP* 62.

The story of Atlantis and Athens, about to be recalled by Critias, goes back to his childhood memories—all the way back to a time when he was only ten years old: his grandfather Critias, whose namesake he is, had told him the story on a day of initiation, Koureotis Day, during the Feast of Apatouria (21a–b).[34] As a ten-year-old, however, Critias would have been too young to be initiated, and this detail about his under-age status underlines the inherent childishness of the listener.[35] In this specific context, Plato adds an interesting further detail that reinforces the idea of childish perceptions: on Koureotis Day, Critias reminisces, he and his little friends used to engage in a very special game. They played rhapsode, competing for prizes, *athla*, arranged by their fathers (ἆθλα γὰρ ἡμῖν οἱ πατέρες ἔθεσαν ῥαψῳδίας 21b). In the general context of the *Timaeus*, the occasion of which is actually the Panathenaia, this mention of *rhapsôidia* is suggestive: it evokes the prime occasion of rhapsodic contests for prizes. This occasion is in fact the Panathenaia.[36] On the occasion of the real Panathenaia, rhapsodes competed—and cooperated—in performing the Homeric *Iliad* and *Odyssey*. On the occasion of that Koureotis Day of long ago, according to Plato's dramatized reminiscences of Critias, the boys were competing in rhapsodic performances of "many poets" (πολλῶν μὲν οὖν δὴ καὶ πολλὰ ἐλέχθη ποιητῶν ποιήματα 21b). Among the "new" poetic compositions of that era, many of the boys "sang" the poems of Solon (ἅτε δὲ νέα κατ᾽ ἐκεῖνον τὸν χρόνον ὄντα τὰ Σόλωνος πολλοὶ τῶν παίδων ᾔσαμεν 21b).[37] Why is Solon highlighted in these reminiscences, and not Homer? Solon's general pertinence to the *Timaeus* is obvious: what this lawmaker had heard from priests in Egypt is suppos-

[34] On the identification of this Critias with the leader of the Thirty, see Clay 1997:52n6.

[35] Brisson 1982:61.

[36] Detienne 1989:178 describes Critias' recalled event as a "little theater of the Apatouria"; it is "une sorte d'antichambre des Panathénées" (ibid.).

[37] On "singing" as applied to the recitative performances of rhapsodes, see *PH* 21, 26.

edly the source of the grandfather Critias' story about Athens and Atlantis. Solon's specific pertinence to the Panathenaia, however, is no longer obvious to us. The immediate context of the *Timaeus* will now help provide an explanation.

The poetry of Solon, as we know from the surviving fragments, was composed in elegiac and iambic meters; these two meters, along with the dactylic hexameter, are the three basic "non-lyric" media that rhapsodes specialize in performing, while most other meters belong to the "lyric" media performed by citharodes or aulodes.[38] Solon's status as a composer of rhapsodic poetry is pertinent to the *Timaeus* because he is pointedly compared by the grandfather Critias to Homer and Hesiod themselves: if only Solon had not left unfinished his poetic composition about Atlantis and Athens, says the grandfather, this statesman would have surpassed even Homer and Hesiod in poetic fame (21c–d). If this unfinished poetry of Solon had been performed by rhapsodes at the real Panathenaia, the performers would have become the continuators of a never-ending story.

We may note a formal parallelism of rhapsodic repertoires in Plato's *Ion*: the rhapsode Ion, who is about to compete in the Panathenaia (530b), is represented as a grand master in performing the poetry of Homer and Hesiod, as also of Archilochus (531a). The rhapsode is a master performer—without musical accompaniment (533b5–7)—of dactylic hexameter (Homer and Hesiod) as also of elegiac and iambic meters (both these meters were primary compositional media of Archilochus). From such formal parallelisms, we can see that the poetic medium of Solon—elegiac and iambic meters—is appropriate to the performance repertoire of rhapsodes. Solon's poetry is rhapsodic poetry. But is this poetry appropriate for rhapsodic performance at the Panathenaia?

Plato's *Timaeus* implies that the rhapsodic poetry of Solon could have replaced the rhapsodic poetry of Homer at the

---

[38] Extended discussion in *PH* 25–28.

Panathenaia, if only the great Athenian statesman had found the leisure time to finish his unfinished poem about Atlantis and Athens (21c–d). By further implication, the rhapsodic tale told by grandfather Critias could have become the poetic centerpiece of the Panathenaia. But Solon did not complete his rhapsodic masterpiece—just as Plato did not complete his trilogy of *Timaeus*, *Critias*, and *Hermocrates*. As I will now go on to argue, this state of incompleteness is expressed by Plato in a nostalgically playful way, and the playfulness cleverly mimics the childish mentality of a ten-year-old boy playing at a game of rhapsodes, where the object of the game is to win celebrity status as the star rhapsode of the Panathenaia.

Critias looks back at those early days when he and the other children playing rhapsode had not yet become eligible to enter the "real" world of grownups. Now, in the *Timaeus* and the *Critias*, we find the adult Critias still at it—playing rhapsode on the occasion of the Panathenaia. Plato's wording of Critias' reminiscences leaves the impression that Critias' game is still in some ways a children's game.[39]

In the *Timaeus*, which features the *dramatis personae* of Socrates, Timaeus, Critias, and Hermocrates, we find references to the subject-matter of an encounter of the same dramatis personae that had taken place "yesterday," *khthes* (17c, 26c, etc.). The subject-matter of "yesterday" had concerned an ideal city-state or republic (*politeia*: 17c, etc.), and Socrates had talked about them "yesterday" in the form of a *muthos* (ἐν μύθῳ: 26c, etc.). These references in the *Timaeus* are cross-references, it would seem, to Plato's *Republic*, which begins with a highlighted reference to *khthes* 'yesterday' (κατέβην χθὲς εἰς τὸν Πειραιᾶ: 327a). And yet, the *khthes* 'yesterday' of the *Timaeus*

---

[39] Compare *Timaeus* 22b: the Egyptians tell Solon that he and all the Greeks are mere children, since their myths (as recounted to them by Solon) are so "new" in comparison to the far more ancient myths recovered in the Egyptian records. Thus the story of Atlantis, as recounted to Solon by the Egyptians, has been filtered through the perspective of a "child" when Solon in turn recounts the story to the Greeks.

involves the dramatis personae of the *Timaeus*, not the *dramatis personae* of the *Republic* (Socrates, Kephalos, Thrasymachus, and so on).[40] So we cannot say that the *Timaeus* cross-refers to the "real" *Republic*.

What we can say, however, is that the *Timaeus* fictionalizes the *Republic*, since we do know for a fact that a "real" *Republic* exists—if indeed we have already read it. Plato's *Timaeus* is marked throughout by the genre of "fiction"—that is, of εἰκὼς λόγος (*eikôs logos*: e.g. 48a, 53d).[41] Since Plato knows that we know fiction when we see it, if indeed we have read the "real" *Republic* carefully, he cannot expect us to take the *khthes* literally.

In the interplay of cross-reference, the fact that the word *khthes* is consistently juxtaposed with *politeia* 'republic' in the *Timaeus* may be viewed, in and of itself, as a reference to the *Republic*, in light of the prominent featuring of that word at the beginning of the *Republic*. For the reference to be a cross-reference, you do not have to reconcile the logic of the immediate context with the logic of the ultimate context, which controls the ultimate purpose of reference.

In terms of the immediate context of the *Timaeus*, its own dramatic moment is the eve of the Panathenaia, which started on the 28th of the month Hekatombaion. By contrast, the dramatic moment of the *Republic* was the feast of the Bendideia, which started on the 19th of the month Thargelion. Recognizing the dramatic moment of the *Republic*, Proclus infers that the dramatic moment of the *Timaeus* must have been the 20th of Thargelion—that is, the day after the *Republic*. In other words, Proclus is taking the usage of *khthes* 'yesterday' in the *Timaeus* as a historical reference to the setting of the *Republic*. At the

---

[40] See Hadot 1983:122n57.

[41] On *eikôs logos* as a genre (*Gattung*), see Witte 1964, who emphasizes an interesting constraint in Plato's usage: the term *eikôs logos* is avoided in the many references to the central *muthos* about Atlantis.

same time, he does not want to let go of the immediate context of the *Timaeus*, from which he infers that the feast in question is indeed the Panathenaia.

Proclus attempts to reason his way out of such contradictions by conjecturing that the feast in question is not the Greater Panathenaia, held every four years, but the Lesser Panathenaia, held on each of the other three years. He is guessing that the Lesser Panathenaia in Athens were held in the month of Thargelion, the same time when the Bendideia were held at the Peiraieus. Here he gets caught in a mistake from the standpoint of modern scholars, who have access to more evidence about the scheduling of the Panathenaia in the fifth and fourth centuries BCE than did Proclus, who lived almost a millennium later, in the fifth century CE.[42]

Such a mistake is really a mistake only if we follow Proclus in assuming that the dramatic dates of the *Republic* and the *Timaeus* need to be connected historically. For Plato, however, I submit that any intended thematic connection between the *Republic* and the *Timaeus* is purely literary, not historical: the Republic of "yesterday" had dealt with the topic of the ideal state, while the *Timaeus* of "today" announces a new topic, that is, a state that must be pure fiction.

That seems as far as we can go in looking for intertextual connections between different works of Plato. It is self-defeating to attempt to go further, as Proclus did, by seeking connections between the internal consistencies of one distinct work of Plato with those of another.[43] Platonic cross-reference cannot be expected to impose an overall sense of order on any single work from the cumulative totality of the outside. Still, my point remains that the usage of *khthes* 'yesterday' in the *Timaeus* is a case of partial intertextuality, that is, where a cross-reference in

---

[42] Cf. Hadot 1983:117, with bibliography. Also Clay 1997:50–51.

[43] For more on the esoteric outlook of Proclus, see Loraux 1993:176 and 434n16.

one given work of Plato to another does not interfere with the individual philosophical and literary agenda of either work.[44] The intentionality of this kind of intertextuality is reflected, I submit, in Plato's use of the language of rhapsodes. From what I am about to show, it appears that Plato is making a point about individualized rhapsodic style and even individualized rhapsodic content, within the framework of an imposed and previously-agreed-upon sequence of narrative. When it is Critias' turn in the *Critias* to take up where Timaeus in the *Timaeus* had left off, Timaeus says: "I hand over [*paradidomen*] to Critias, as prearranged, the continuous discourse [*ephexês logos*]" (*Critias* 106b: παραδίδομεν κατὰ τὰς ὁμολογίας Κριτίᾳ τὸν ἐφεξῆς λόγον). I draw attention here to the expression *ephexês logos* 'continuous discourse'. We may compare the rhapsodic expression *ephexês* in the earlier passage quoted in my essay, in "Plato" *Hipparkhos* 228b–c.

Critias responds by saying that he will now "take up the continuous discourse" at the point where it was handed over to him by Timaeus. I draw attention to the precise wording: *dekhomai* 'I take up', with the direct object *ephexês logos* 'continuous discourse' understood. The whole idea is worded in a noticeably compressed clause marked by the particle *men,* to be followed by an expanded clause, marked by the particle *de,* which expresses the idea that the discourse will now become

---

[44] Similarly with the *Timaeus* and the *Critias*. These two works are much more closely connected with each other than the *Republic* is connected with the *Timaeus* (it can be argued, as we will see below, that they are not even separate works), and yet even in this case we may find individual consistencies. For example, the presiding god of the *Timaeus* is Athena, who is also the primary designated subject of the narration, which takes the form of "hymn," *humnos* (21a: τὴν θεὸν...ὑμνοῦντας), while the gods of the *Critias* are Apollo/Paeon and the Muses, who are invoked to preside over the next designated subject, "the ancient and noble citizens" of prehistoric Athens, and again the narration takes the form of "hymn," *humnos* (108c: τὸν Παίωνά τε καὶ τὰς Μούσας ἐπικαλούμενον τοὺς παλαιοὺς πολίτας ἀγαθοὺς ὄντας ἀναφαίνειν τε καὶ ὑμνεῖν). Here too, intertextuality need not prevent individual textuality in *Timaeus* / *Critias*.

even more challenging than before, and that the speaker must therefore beg the indulgence of his audience all the more: ἀλλ᾽ ὦ Τίμαιε δέχομαι μέν· ᾧ δὲ καὶ κατ᾽ ἀρχὰς σὺ ἐχρήσω, συγγνώμην αἰτούμενος ὡς περὶ μεγάλων μέλλων λέγειν, ταὐτὸν καὶ νῦν ἐγὼ τοῦτο παραιτοῦμαι ... 'all right, then, Timaeus, I'm taking it up [dekhomai] here [that is, the continuous discourse], on the one hand [men]; on the other hand [de], I ask for the very same thing that you too made use of at the beginning when you asked for indulgence on the grounds that you were about to speak about great [megala] things' (Critias 106b–c). Critias goes on to say that his subject matter is surely even greater (106c).

The usage of the verb dekhomai 'take up' in this context (106b) is crucial. We may compare the participle of this same verb as applied to Patroklos at Iliad IX 191: he sits in a state of anticipation, "waiting" (δέγμενος) for the moment when Achilles will leave off (verb lêgô) singing the klea andrôn 'glories of heroes'. As I have argued, Patroklos is apparently waiting for his own turn to sing, and what we see here in capsule form is "the esthetics of rhapsodic sequencing."[45] The verb lêgô 'leave off' is elsewhere attested in explicitly rhapsodic contexts, as in the following passage:

τά τε Ὁμήρου ἐξ ὑποβολῆς γέγραφε ῥαψῳδεῖσθαι, οἷον ὅπου ὁ πρῶτος ἔληξεν, ἐκεῖθεν ἄρχεσθαι τὸν ἐχόμενον

He [= Solon the Lawgiver][46] has written a law that the works of Homer are to be performed rhapsodically

---

[45] See again PP 73.

[46] On the interchangeability of Solon / Peisistratos in the charter myth of the "lawgiver" who integrates the heretofore disintegrated corpus of Homeric poetry, see the discussion in Ch. 1.

[*rhapsôideô*], by <u>relay</u> [*hupobolê*], so that wherever the first person <u>left off</u> [*lêgô*], from that point the next <u>connected</u> person should <u>start</u>.

Dieuchidas of Megara FGH 485 F 6
via Diogenes Laertius 1.57[47]

Critias remarks that his topic, the genesis of humans, is even more difficult than the topic that had just been treated by Timaeus, the genesis of the gods and of the cosmos, since the audience will demand greater verisimilitude about topics that seem closer to their own world of direct experience (107a–b). Socrates jokingly responds that the topic of the next slated speaker, Hermocrates, will surely become even more difficult (108a–b).

Of course, Plato's readers will never get to see even the beginnings of Hermocrates' topic, since the sequence of a would-be trilogy of *Timaeus*, *Critias*, and *Hermocrates* is cut short well before even the *Critias* can come to a finish. An obvious inference, then, is that Plato never finished his intended trilogy.[48] There is, however, also a less obvious inference that could be drawn: perhaps Plato intended the sequence of *Timaeus* / *Critias* to remain unfinished.[49] In support of this

---

[47] Cf. Ford 1992:115 n31, who notes the use of *lêgô* 'stop, leave off' at the point in the narrative where Demodokos leaves off his Trojan narrative (*Odyssey* viii 87); this verb, Ford argues, "is the technical expression used by a rhapsode to end a performance or a part of one." For parallels, he cites *Homeric Hymn to Dionysus* 17–18, Hesiod fr. 305.4 MW, and *Theogony* 48. He also cites Diogenes Laertius 1.57 [Dieuchidas of Megara FGH 485 F 6] and *Iliad* IX 191, the two passages presently under discussion.

[48] Cf. Plutarch *Life of Solon* 31.3, 32.1–2.

[49] Cf. Clay 1997. See also Haslam 1976, who argues that *Timaeus* + *Critias* are really one unfinished dialogue; he makes a similar argument about the *Sophist* + *Statesman*, discounting the idea that Plato intentionally sets up the expectation of a trilogy comprised of *Sophist* + *Statesman* (+ *Philosopher*), which would be parallel to *Timaeus* + *Critias* (+ *Hermocrates*). In what follows, I argue that Plato did indeed intentionally set up the expectation of a sequence *Timaeus* + *Critias* + *Hermocrates*.

inference, we may point to the open-endedness that typifies Plato's dialectic in general.[50]

Critias' speech stops short at exactly the point where he is about to quote the Will of Zeus (δίκην αὐτοῖς ἐπιθεῖναι βουληθείς 121b–c). Plato's wording evokes the epic theme of the *boulê* or 'Will' of Zeus, as announced at the very beginning of the *Iliad*, I 5 (Διὸς δ' ἐτελείετο βουλή) or at the very beginning of the *Cypria* fr. 1.7 Allen (Διὸς δ' ἐτελείετο βουλή). At the point where Critias' speech stops short, Zeus is about to announce that he will now inflict a Flood on the Golden Generation—the last of a doomed race who have finally exhausted their divine genetic destiny (*moira*) because of their habitual interbreeding with ordinary mortals (*Critias* 121c). This point of stopping short, I argue, is analogous to a given point in epic narrative where one rhapsode could leave off the narration and another rhapsode could take it up.

In support of this argument, I draw attention to two points in the overall narrative of the *Iliad*: one of them comes at the end of Book VIII, and the other at the end of Book XV. As Bruce Heiden points out, both Books VIII and XV end on a note of asserting the *boulê* or "Will" of Zeus.[51] Heiden argues that both endings seem to signal major breaks in the performance of the *Iliad*. In stressing the factor of performance, not just composition, he is following the theory of Oliver Taplin, who posits three successive units or "movements" in three successive nights for the actual performing of the *Iliad*: I–IX, X–XVIII 353, XVIII 354–XXIV.[52] Heiden modifies this theory by positing a different set of divisions for the three "movements," which he thinks were performed in three *days* rather than nights: *Iliad* I–VIII, IX–XV, XVI–XXIV.[53] He argues that these posited divisions in the course of Iliadic performance were meant to mark points of sus-

---

[50] See especially Dihle 1995.

[51] Heiden 1996:19–22.

[52] Taplin 1992:11–31.

[53] Heiden 1996:21.

pense, not of resolution: at the end of both VIII and XV, the Will of Zeus is being asserted at a moment when the outcome of the overall plot seems as yet undecided.[54]

I agree with Heiden's specific inference that these major divisions at the endings of *Iliad* VIII and XV are compositional as well as performative. I also agree with his general inference that the endings of all Homeric "books" are likewise both compositional and performative.[55] As I have argued in my earlier work, the division of the Homeric *Iliad* and *Odyssey* into twenty-four "books" (a better word would be "scrolls") stems from distinctly *rhapsodic* traditions of performance, and even the traditional word for designating one of these "books," *rhapsôidia*, reflects the technical language of rhapsodic practice.[56]

I disagree, however, with the position taken by Heiden when he argues that the divisions of the *Iliad* and *Odyssey* into twenty-four books "were designed and textualized by the composer himself."[57] I also disagree with the position taken by Taplin on the other extreme: he argues not only that the book-divisions "do not go back to the formation of the poems" but also that they are relatively recent, probably the work of Alexandrian scholars.[58] The major narrative breaks that Taplin posits for the

---

[54] I do not agree with other aspects of Heiden's argumentation, especially the idea that the Will of Zeus is in each of these two cases a "counter-assertion" to the will of Achilles, and that this counter-assertion is expressed programmatically already in *Iliad* I 1–5 (p. 21). Zeus wills the realization of the *mênis* 'anger' of Achilles, not its thwarting, at *Iliad* I 5. See *BA* 1979 Ch. 20, where I offer an extended discussion of the synchronization of the Will of Zeus with the plot and the imagery of the *Iliad*. It surprises me to read the claim of Heiden 1997:222n5 that "Nagy says little about the gods" (also p. 223n9). When he quotes me (p. 223) as saying that "the praise of Homeric poetry is restricted to the heroes of the distant past" (*PH* 150), he does not note the context of my formulation: I am contrasting these heroes of the past with the audience in the here-and-now of Homeric performance. On the subject of divine models for epic praise, see *PH* 359–361.

[55] Heiden 1998.

[56] *PP* 181–183 (68, 79).

[57] Heiden 1998:82. For a position similar to Heiden's, see Stanley 1993.

[58] Taplin 1992:285.

Iliad are more distinct, he contends, than the breaks separating the Books of the *Iliad* as we know them.[59]

As an alternative to these positions, I offer here an intermediate formulation, based on an evolutionary model for the making of Homeric poetry.[60] In terms of such a model, I have argued, "what may be a three-part division in one stage of the tradition, which is what Taplin posits for the *Iliad*, may not necessarily be incompatible with a 24-part division at another stage."[61] These "divisions," I should stress, are not *textual* in terms of my formulation: rather, they are simultaneously *compositional* and *performative*. That is, they are aspects of a process of recomposition, evolving over time in the historical contexts of each reperformance. In short, "I hold open the possibility that the eventual division of the *Iliad* and *Odyssey* each into twenty-four Books results from the cumulative formation of episodes in the process of equalized or even weighting."[62]

Having noted my disagreements with Heiden's formulation of performative breaks in Homeric poetry, I return to a central point of agreement, concerning the suspenseful endings of *Iliad* VIII and XV. So far, we have seen that the effect of suspense is achieved by way of breaking the narrative at a point where the Will of Zeus is not yet fully realized. The choosing of such points for breaking the narrative, I have been arguing, reflects a distinctly rhapsodic practice. Further, I have been comparing these points for breaking the Homeric narrative with the point in Plato's *Critias* where the text breaks off, at the precise moment when the Will of Zeus is about to be quoted directly.

The analogy seems incomplete, however, since the Will of Zeus, as spoken in his own words, is "quoted" in *Iliad* VIII

---

[59] Taplin pp. 285–293.

[60] *HQ* Ch. 3–4; *PP* Ch. 5–7.

[61] *HQ* 88n72.

[62] *HQ* 88; on the concept of "equalized weighting," see *HQ* 77–82. As I remark in *HQ* 88, "It is from a diachronic point of view that I emphasize the *cumulative* formation of episodes in the *process* of even weighting."

and XV not at the end of these "books" but further back (VIII 470–483 and XV 14–33, 49–77). Still, the actual effects of the words spoken by Zeus are suspensefully held back by the narrative of each of these "books," all the way to the very end of each.

The analogy becomes clearer if we trace the overall metaphorical world of the Will of Zeus in the *Iliad*. From *Iliad* I through *Iliad* XV, as I have argued at length elsewhere, the Will of Zeus is visualized as an archetypal Conflagration inflicted by the thunderbolt of Zeus, and this visualization is applied metaphorically to the fire of Hektor as it threatens to destroy the ships of the Achaeans.[63] In terms of the overall plot of the *Iliad*, if the fire of Hektor had burned down the ships of the Achaeans, these seafaring ancestors of the Hellenes would all have perished, and Hellenic civilization itself would have become extinct.[64] This extinction, had it happened, would have been caused immediately by the fire of Hektor—but ultimately by a Conflagration sent by the Will of Zeus.

Fortunately for the Achaeans, the Will of Zeus stops short of Conflagration: "for Zeus, the *selas* 'flash' of Hektor's fire at XV 600 signals the termination of the Trojan onslaught, which was inaugurated by the *selas* of his own thunderstroke at VIII 76."[65] The Trojans will not be so fortunate: from *Iliad* XV 600 onward, the Will of Zeus will start to turn against them, and the rest of the plot of the *Iliad* will lead inexorably toward their own ultimate extinction by way of Conflagration.

This Homeric theme of ultimate extinction is pertinent to the themes of Plato's *Timaeus* and *Critias*. Already in the *Timaeus*, we see a polar opposition between two kinds of eschatological disaster, that is, Conflagration (Ecpyrosis) and Flood (Cataclysm): the first is exemplified by the myth of Phaethon (22c) and the second, by the myth of Deukalion (22a). At the

---

[63] *BA* 334–347. Cf. also Muellner 1996.

[64] *BA* 338.

[65] *BA* 336.

point where the *Critias* breaks off, the Will of Zeus is about to unleash the second kind of eschatological disaster, the Cataclysm.

In the *Iliad*, the alternative eschatological themes of Ecpyrosis and Cataclysm are in fact both applied: the first threatens both the Trojans and the Achaeans, while the second threatens only the Achaeans.[66] Either way, the essential fact remains: Ecpyrosis and Cataclysm are the visible epic manifestations of the Will of Zeus.

In sum, the *Critias* of Plato breaks off at a point that corresponds to a break in rhapsodic performance. What then, could this correspondence tell us about the narrative sequence of the *Timaeus* and *Critias*?

In the wording of the *Timaeus*, the narrative about Atlantis was told to Solon *hexês* 'in sequence' (23d) by the Egyptian priests, after they had re-read their own written record *ephexês* 'in sequence' (24a). The contexts of these terms *hexês / ephexês* are analogous to the context of *ephexês logos* 'continuous discourse' in *Critias* 106b, which I have already compared to the overtly rhapsodic context of *ephexês* in "Plato" *Hipparkhos* 228b–c. As we have seen, the context of *Critias* 106b is in fact likewise overtly rhapsodic. When it is Critias' turn in the *Critias* to take up where Timaeus in the *Timaeus* had left off, Timaeus says: "I hand over [*paradidomen*] to Critias, as prearranged, the continuous discourse [*ephexês logos*]" (*Critias* 106b: παραδίδομεν κατὰ τὰς ὁμολογίας Κριτίᾳ τὸν ἐφεξῆς λόγον).

The problem is, Critias can never finish narrating this "continuous discourse," just as Solon never finished turning this narrative into his own poetry in the first place. If only Solon had not left unfinished his poetic composition about Atlantis and Athens, says the grandfather, this statesman would have sur-

[66] Rousseau 1996:403–413, 591–592, with special reference to the stylized Cataclysm of *Iliad* XII 17–33 and the Battle of Fire and Water in *Iliad* XXI 211–327 (on which see also *HQ* 145–146).

passed even Homer and Hesiod in poetic fame (*Timaeus* 21c–d). If only Solon had finished, his Atlantis would have become the "continuous discourse" of rhapsodes.

The discontinuity of the Atlantis narrative highlights the openendedness of the narrative sequence from the *Timaeus* to the *Critias* to the nonexistent *Hermocrates*. The break in continuity happens at a point in the narrative when the narration has some time ago shifted from gods to humans: that shift is signaled already at the beginning of the speech of Critias (*Critias* 107a–b). That this speech is seemingly meant to address purely human affairs, not divine, is underlined by Plato's evocative references to the world of history. When Critias describes his whole speech as *parakhrêma legomena* 'things spoken with reference to the present contingencies' (107d–e)—his wording evokes the passage in Thucydides 1.22.4 where the historian rejects the ephemeral preoccupations of his predecessors (ἀγώνισμα ἐς τὸ παραχρῆμα ἀκούειν 'a competitive occasion meant for hearing with reference to the present [historical] contingencies' [*parakhrêma*]). Later on, when Critias describes the *moira* 'destiny' of golden-age humanity as *exitêlos* 'extinct' (*Critias* 121a), his wording evokes the beginning of the *History* of Herodotus, where the historian expresses his ultimate intent to rescue human affairs from becoming *exitêla* 'extinct' (Herodotus *prooemium*).[67]

It is precisely at this moment in the narrative of the *Critias* that the Will of Zeus is about to reassert itself in the course of human affairs. It is also precisely at this moment that Zeus, just as he begins to speak, is precluded from uttering even one word. How ineffable of Zeus even to try to speak at this

---

[67] For a related evocation of the prooemium of Herodotus in *Timaeus* 20e, see *PH* 226. By implication, Plato's *Timaeus* is a monumental *prooemium* or *humnos* in its own right: see again see n33 above. The genetic implications of *exitêlos* at the end of the *Critias*, 121a, where the *moira* 'destiny' of the golden generation becomes *exitêlos* 'extinct' precisely because of their "mixing" their genes with ordinary mortals, can be compared with the context of *exitêlos* in Herodotus 5.39.2, with reference to the extinction of a genetic line. Cf. *PH* 225.

point in the flow of narration, given that the dialogue of Critias had already started off by shifting from divine to human affairs!

The open-endedness of the narrative sequence from the *Timaeus* to the *Critias* to the nonexistent *Hermocrates* leaves no chance for Hermocrates, described as *tritos* (*Critias* 108a6), even to start—let alone finish. If he had indeed started, Hermocrates would have needed "a second beginning," *hetera arkhê*, in any case (*Critias* 108b). That way, he would not have had to resort to the same old beginning, *arkhê*.

Before Critias gets to have his own beginning, *arkhê*, Socrates jokingly prophesies for him the fate that befalls those who compete in the world of theater, referring to what he calls the "mentality" of that medium (literally, its *dianoia* 'train of thought': τὴν τοῦ θεάτρου διάνοιαν): the "previous poet" (ὁ πρότερος ... ποιητής), he says, will always have a big advantage (*Critias* 108b).[68]

At this point, Hermocrates responds to Socrates that "we" must bravely move ahead, that is, that Critias as the second in the sequence of three speakers must bravely move ahead and start his speech (*Critias* 108c). Critias responds by expressing his admiration for these brave but doomed words of Hermocrates, who is "last in line" (τῆς ὑστέρας τεταγμένος) and, worse, who still "has someone else in front of him," someone who has not yet even performed for his audience (ἐπίπροσθεν ἔχων ἄλλον *Critias* 108c). At this moment, Critias refers to his present audience as "this theater" (τῷδε τῷ θεάτρῳ 108d).[69]

---

[68] Here I see an explicit merger of the imagery of rhapsodes competing in the festival of the Panathenaia with the imagery of poets competing in theatrical festivals like the Dionysia. Plato indulges in such mergers of images, especially in the *Ion*. In *HR*, I examine more closely the parallelisms in Plato's references to rhapsodic and theatrical competitions in light of historical evidence for parallelisms in the evolution of *rhapsôidoi* 'rhapsodes' and *hupokritai* 'actors'.

[69] On "theater" as the audience of rhapsodes, see again the previous note. Note that *theatai* 'theater-goers' refers to the audiences of rhapsodes at *Ion* 535d8.

As I contemplate Hermocrates in his role of the potential *tritos* (108a6), I see a failed sequence of three would-be rhapsodes: Timaeus, Critias, Hermocrates. If these three *dramatis personae* had succeeded in putting it all together, we would have had three rhapsodes performing some kind of poetic totality for one day. "Yesterday" there was another set of performances, adding up to a fictional equivalent of the *Republic*.[70] "Today," the sequence of would-be rhapsodes does not quite add up— unless perhaps the reader is able to take the place of Hermocrates in this ongoing rhapsody.

---

[70] The potential totality of *Timaeus* +*Critias* + *Hermocrates* may be the equivalent, in rhapsodic terms, of one of three "movements" in the performance of the *Iliad*. In terms of the three performative "movements" of the *Iliad*, as Taplin 1992:21n20 argues, cross-references in one given "movement" to the previous "movement" can be worded in terms of "yesterday." That is, "yesterday" can refer to yesterday's *performance*, not to an event that happened yesterday in terms of the narrative per se. In XIII 745, for example, χθιζὸν χρεῖος 'debt of yesterday' refers to the Trojan victory of Book VIII. See in general Taplin p. 21 for other possible examples.

Chapter 3
Humnos in Homer and Plato:
Weaving the Robe of the Goddess[1]

Pursuing an evolutionary model for the making of Homeric poetry, I have argued that this "making" needs to be seen diachronically as well as synchronically. An unexplored aspect of this "making" is "textualizing." To develop the idea of textualization, let us turn to the metaphorical world of the Greek word *humnos*. We need to consider not so much the etymology but the technical meaning of this word—as it was used in its technical sense by poets and rhetoricians. To translate the word by way of its modern derivative, "hymn," obscures that sense. From the technical viewpoint of poets and rhetoricians, *humnos* is not just a "hymn"—that is, a song sung in praise of gods or heroes—but also a song that functions as a connector, a continuator. It converges with the idea of the *prooimion*, but that word too has a sense that goes beyond our ordinary translation as "proem" or "prelude." Technically, both *humnos* and *prooimion* have to do with the general idea of an authoritative beginning that makes continuity possible. More specifically, as we see in the usage of Homeric poetry and of Plato as an avid listener of Homeric poetry, the *humnos* is not just a proem that introduces epic but also the sequencing principle that connects with epic, then extends into epic, and then finally becomes the same thing as epic itself.

My starting-point is the expression ἀοιδῆς ὕμνον 'humnos of song' at *Odyssey* viii 429. This expression conveys the idea of the *totality* of a given performance of a song.[2] The noun *humnos* can be explained as a derivative of the verb-root that we

---

[1]The original version of this essay is N 2001a.

[2] *PP* 64n22, following Koller 1956:177 on *humnos* as used at the final lines of attested Homeric Hymns; cf. *PH* 354n77 and *GM* 54n56.

see in *huphainô* 'weave', in the metaphorical sense of 'web' or 'fabric' of song; an attractive alternative explanation is that *humnos* is related to *humên*—more specifically, that *humnos* and *humên* are both derived from another word for fabric-working, the verb-root **syuH-* 'sew'.[3] The actual derivation, however, is less important than the facts of usage. The point is, metaphors referring to the craft of fabric-workers pervade the usage of *humnos* in archaic Greek poetics. My central argument is that the word *humnos* is related to a metaphor that likens the fabric-worker to the *rhapsôidos* 'rhapsode', the etymology of which can be explained as 'he who sews together the song(s)'.[4] I say "fabric-worker" instead of "weaver" in order to include various kinds of specialized fabric production, not just weaving, in the overall historical context of the Greek-speaking world in the second millennium BCE and thereafter.[5] Such a differentiation, I argue, is reflected metaphorically in the word for 'rhapsode', *rhapsôidos*, in the etymological sense of 'he who sews together the song(s)'. In other words, the metaphor inherent in this word implies the existence of professional male fabric-workers.[6] The

---

[3] In her 1996 thesis, Diana Gibson has adduced both linguistic and thematic evidence to show that *humên* is indeed derived from the root-verb **syuH-*, the basic meaning of which has to do with fabric work, and there are no serious phonological problems in deriving *humnos* as well from this root. There are phonological problems with deriving *humnos* from the root of *huphainô*; see *PP* 64-65. But see Schmitt 1967:300, with special reference to the collocation of *huphainô* 'weave' plus *humnos* as its object in Bacchylides *Epinicia* 5.9-10.

[4] For a detailed exploration of the semantics of this word, see *PP* 61–78. Cf. Ford 1988. See also N 1997d on the distinctions between *rhapsôidos* and *aoidos* ('singer'): "No doubt these two words represent relatively earlier and later stages in the prehistory and history of performance traditions"; see *HQ* 75–76, especially n37, with bibliography.

[5] On the differentiation of *sewing* as a specialized aspect of the overall activity of *weaving*, see *PP* 61–76, with reference to the Greek words *rhaptô* and *huphainô* respectively.

[6] See again *PP* 61–76 on the implicit association of the fabric-work designated by *rhaptô* with the work of men in particular. Already in the Linear B documents, the verb *rhaptô* applies to the work of men: see Chadwick and Baumbach 1963:242–243 on the masculine agent-noun ra-pte / ra-pte-re= *rhaptêr* / *rhaptêres*, vs. the feminine ra-pi-ti-ra₂ = *rhaptriai*.

humnos of song at *Odyssey* viii 429, I further argue, reflects metaphorically the workmanship of such artisans.[7] The work of the singer is metaphorically interlaced with the work of the fabric-worker. A prime example is the singer who performs for the Phaeacians, Demodokos, who is described as beginning the first of his three performances in *Odyssey* viii by starting from a thread, *oimê* (viii 74), much as a fabric-worker might.[8] Here we return to the reference at *Odyssey* viii 429 to the *humnos* of Demodokos. What connects the Homeric usage of *humnos* to the idea of weaving is a preoccupation with beginnings. The word *humnos*, as I will now argue, is concerned primarily with the choice of an ad hoc beginning, of an ad hoc point of departure.

When Demodokos starts singing his third song, which is specified as *aoidê*, at viii 499, he starts with a god, the identity of whom is not specified by the narrative: *hormêtheis theou arkheto* 'getting started, he began with the god'. What follows this start, as we hear it paraphrased by the *Odyssey*, is an epic account of the Iliou Persis, the destruction of Troy (viii 500–520). The reinforcing expression *hormêtheis* 'getting started' at viii 499 has to do with the singer's point of departure: the verb *hormaô* is derived from the noun *hormê*, aptly described as "le seul véritable dérivé de *ornumi*";[9] *hormê* can mean 'setting oneself in motion', as at the start of marching (LSJ s.v., III); I note the compound *aphormê*, which actually means 'point of departure' (cf. *aphormêthentos* at II 794, ii 375, iv 748).

---

[7] See especially Sophocles *Epigonoi* fr. 771 Radt, as supplemented by *Pap.Oxy.* inv. 87/110(a), to be published by Ch. Mülke, Corpus Christi College (also by H. Lloyd-Jones): we now have an attestation of a masculine agent noun *huphantêres* 'weavers' (col. ii line 8: ὑφαντῆ[ρες]).

[8] On the interpretation of *oimê* as 'thread' at viii 74, see *PP* 63n19, n20. In a future project, I hope to show that *oimos* in the sense of 'way' is a metaphorical extension of the idea of 'thread'.

[9] Chantraine *DELG* 823.

The expression *theou arkheto* 'he began with the god' at viii 499 indicates that Demodokos is singing a *humnos*. In the Homeric Hymns, which refer to themselves explicitly as *humnos* (as in the expression *metabêsomai allon es humnon* at *HH* 5.293, 9.9, 18.11, to be discussed below), the point of departure is marked by the collocation of *arkhomai* 'I begin' with the name of the specified god in the genitive (*HH* 4.293, 9.8, 18.11, 31.18, 32.18).[10] From the standpoint of the Homeric *humnos*—*as a performance*—the god who is specified as the point of departure thereby presides over that performance *in its entirety*. The *humnos* is not just the beginning of the performance: everything that follows the *humnos* becomes part of the *humnos*, by virtue of the invoked god's authority. The concept of *arkhê* is not just a matter of beginnings: it is also a matter of authority. Even if a given *humnos*, as a performance that started off with the subject of a god, switches from that subject to some other subject, such as the exploits of heroes, that performance is still notionally a *humnos* because it started as a *humnos*.[11]

It is a mistake, I propose, to assume that the textual endings of extant Homeric Hymns are also their performative endings. The expression *metabêsomai allon es humnon* (*HH* 5.293, 9.9, 18.11) means not, as is commonly thought, 'I will switch to another *humnos*' but rather 'I will switch to the rest of the *humnos*'.[12] If an epic performance is introduced by a *humnos*, then epic becomes part of the *humnos*. Technically, only an epic that fails to be introduced by a *humnos* is not a *humnos*. The *Iliad* and *Odyssey* fit the category of non-*humnos* only if we imagine them as texts that start where we see them starting when we read Scroll One Verse One. It is a mistake, I propose, to assume that the

---

[10] See Koller 1956:190n1.

[11] See Koller 1956:180 on the ending of *HH* 31, verse 19, where the *erga* 'deeds' of *hêmitheoi* 'heroes' are made explicit as the subject of the "main part" of the performance, as Koller puts it.

[12] *PH* p. 353, following Koller 1956.

textual beginnings of the *Iliad* and *Odyssey* are the only possible performative beginnings. [13]

This is not to say that the semantics of *humnos* did not ultimately get extricated from the idea of wholeness. It is precisely by way of *extrication from wholeness* that we arrive, ultimately, at the narrower meaning of "hymn" as we use the word nowadays.

Let us return, however, to the earlier standpoint as reflected by archaic Greek poetry. From this standpoint, the semantics of *humnos* are inextricably connected to the idea of wholeness, which in turn is connected to the idea of an absolutizing *point of departure*. In terms of these connections, we may say that a beginning—wherever that beginning may be—must have a continuum that follows it, producing a whole. The wholeness of the *humnos*, as performance, is marked by the beginning. It is authorized by the beginning. Its *arkhê* is both beginning and authorization. This idea, implicit in *humnos*, of wholeness *as marked by an authoritative beginning* is remarkably similar to Aristotle's idea of *sustasis* 'order' in the plots of tragedies.

Aristotle in the *Poetics* examines the minimum requirement of plot in tragedy, that is, *wholeness* of action, in terms of four aspects of *wholeness:* (1) order = *sustasis*, (2) amplitude, (3) unity, and (4) probable and necessary connection. Let us focus on the first of these aspects, order = *sustasis*:

κεῖται δὴ ἡμῖν τὴν τραγῳδίαν τελείας καὶ ὅλης πράξεως εἶναι μίμησιν ἐχούσης τι μέγεθος· ἔστιν γὰρ ὅλον καὶ μηδὲν ἔχον μέγεθος. ὅλον δέ ἐστιν τὸ ἔχον ἀρχὴν καὶ μέσον καὶ τελευτήν. ἀρχὴ δέ ἐστιν ὃ αὐτὸ μὲν μὴ ἐξ ἀνάγκης μετ᾽ ἄλλο ἐστίν, μετ᾽

---

[13] In N 1998a:217–218, I argue that the beginnings of the *Iliad* and the *Odyssey* (I 1ff and i 1ff), as transmitted in the medieval textual tradition, are technically *without* hymnic *prooimia*. The *prooimia* of the *Iliad* and the *Odyssey*, as we have them, are still *prooimia*, but they are non-hymnic.

ἐκεῖνο δ᾽ ἕτερον πέφυκεν εἶναι ἢ γίνεσθαι· τελευτὴ δὲ τοὐναντίον ὃ αὐτὸ μὲν μετ᾽ ἄλλο πέφυκεν εἶναι ἢ ἐξ ἀνάγκης ἢ ὡς ἐπὶ τὸ πολύ, μετὰ δὲ τοῦτο ἄλλο οὐδέν· μέσον δὲ ὃ καὶ αὐτὸ μετ᾽ ἄλλο καὶ μετ᾽ μήθ᾽ ὁπόθεν ἔτυχεν ἄρχεσθαι μήθ᾽ ὅπου ἔτυχε τελευτᾶν, ἀλλὰ κεχρῆσθαι ταῖς εἰρημέναις ἰδέαις.

Now, we have settled that a tragedy is a *mimêsis* of a complete, that is, of a whole action, 'whole' here implying some amplitude (there can be a whole without amplitude). By 'whole' I mean 'with a beginning, a middle, and an end'. By 'beginning' [in this context] I mean 'that which is not necessarily the consequent of something else, but has some state or happening naturally consequent on it', by 'end' 'a state that is the necessary or usual consequent of something else, but has itself no such consequent', by 'middle' 'that which is consequent and has consequents'. Well-ordered plots, then, will exhibit these characteristics, and will not begin or end just anywhere.

Aristotle *Poetics* Ch. 7 1450b
tr. Hubbard 1972, p. 100

What I find striking about this definition is the emphasis on the fact of sequence, by way of the consequent:

> The beginning has a consequent after it but no consequent before it.
> The middle has a consequent before it and a consequent after it.
> The end has a consequent before it but no consequent after it.

To put it another way:

The beginning may or may not be a consequent and has a consequent after it.

The middle is a consequent and has a consequent before it and a consequent after it.

The end has a consequent before it but no consequent after it.

Unlike the middle and the end, which both have to be a consequent, the beginning does not. The beginning *may* be a consequent, even though it has no consequent before it, but it does not *have* to be a consequent itself. To this extent, the beginning is potentially absolute.

The idea that a *humnos* is an absolute beginning that makes a whole out of everything that follows it is analogous, in terms of my thesis, to the idea of weaving itself. Hereafter I will use this more specific word *weaving* instead of the more general designation *fabric-work*.

Before we proceed, let us review the basic vocabulary of weaving, as we see it described in archaic Greek traditions and elsewhere.[14] *Weaving* is a specialized form of *interlacing* or *plaiting*. The Greek equivalent of *plait* is *plekô*. Whereas *plaiting* is the process of joining basically two sets of whatever element, such as thread, in an over-under-over-under pattern, *weaving* superimposes a frame on this process:

Weaving, in the narrow, technical sense, involves two operationally different sets of elements: a pre-arranged and more-or-less fixed set, the *warp*, and a second set, the *weft* (or *woof*), interlaced into the first set. Weaving differs from plaiting and basketry partly in the differentiation of a weft from a warp, partly in the fixed nature of

---

[14] The following discussion of weaving is an abbreviated version of a more detailed discussion, N 2000b.

the warp, and partly in the extreme length and flexibility of the typical weft.[15]

The frame for these two sets, the *warp* = *chaîne* and the *weft* = *trame*, is the *loom* = *métier*.[16] In the present discussion, I will focus on the single-beam warp-weighted loom,[17] not the ground loom[18] or the vertical two-beam loom.[19] In terms of a warp-weighted loom, which I will hereafter call simply the *loom*, the warp is vertical, hanging from the single beam or crossbeam, and the weft is horizontal. The rod that separates, in an over-under-over-under pattern, the odd/even threads of the warp is the *shed bar* (*shed* is cognate with German *scheiden*).[20] The shed bar guides the *shuttle* = *navette*.[21] Besides the shed bar, there exists a differentiated type of rod known as the *heddle bar*.[22] As for the direction of the whole process, "the weaving started at the top, and the rows of weft had to be packed upwards, against gravity."[23]

Let us now briefly review the pertinent vocabulary in ancient Greek: *histos* is the loom; *stêmôn* or *mitos* designate the vertical threads, = *warp* = *chaîne*, while *krokê* or *rhodanê* designate the horizontal threads, = *weft* = *trame*; *kerkis* is the shuttle.[24] The *kanôn*, as in the description of a weaving woman in *Iliad*

---

[15] Barber 1991:79.

[16] Barber p. 80.

[17] Barber pp. 91–113.

[18] Barber pp. 83–91.

[19] Barber pp. 113–116. The idiosyncrasies of loom traditions in Egypt are connected to the restrictions in raw material used for weaving: unlike elsewhere, the Egyptian tradition concentrates on linen, not wool. See Barber p. 211.

[20] Barber p. 82.

[21] See Barber p. 85n3 on the metaphors inherent in the words *shuttle* and *navette* (imagery of over and under and over and under).

[22] Barber p. 110.

[23] Barber p. 92.

[24] Scheid/Svenbro 1994:21.

XXIII 760–763, is commonly interpreted as a shed bar,[25] though the word may be referring in this context to the more differentiated concept of a heddle bar.[26] The *pênion* is the bobbin or spool that guides, by way of the *kanôn*, the shuttle or *kerkis* over and under and over and under the warp or *mitos*.[27]

Let us also briefly review the pertinent vocabulary in Latin, with special attention to a passage in Ovid *Metamorphoses* 6.53–60 describing the primal weaving contest between the two prototypical female weavers par excellence, Athena and Arachne. The two contestants set up their looms or *têlae*. The threads of the warp or *stâmen* (collective) are stretched vertically, attached from the single beam or crossbeam, that is, *iugum*. The shed or comb is the *harundô*. The thread of the weft, or *subtemen*, is attached to the shuttle or *radius*.[28]

We may note some important semantic convergences and divergences in the Greek. First of all, *huphainô* 'weave' is a specialized kind of *plekô* 'plait', but there are contexts where *plekô* can be used as a synonym of *huphainô*.[29] Also, the process of uniting, by way of weaving, the horizontal warp with the vertical weft is described as *sumplokê* in Plato *Politics* 281a; the same word *sumplokê* describes sexual union in Plato *Symposium* 191c.[30]

Next, let us note some semantic convergences and divergences in English and other languages. Besides the English

---

[25] For example, Richardson 1993:253.

[26] Barber pp. 112, 267.

[27] Barber p. 267 refers to the *pênion* as a weft bobbin. Barber ibid. notes the expression *kata miton* in the sense of 'in due order'. For a semantic parallel, I suggest Latin *ôrdô*.

[28] I note that the woman described as weaving in *Iliad* XXIII 760–63 raises the *kanôn* to the same level as her breasts. This seemingly eroticized detail may be parallel to Ovid *Metamorphoses* 6.59–60: *utraque festinant cinctaeque ad pectora uestes | bracchia docta mouent studio fallente laborem.*

[29] Scheid/Svenbro 1994:35, 126n26.

[30] Scheid/Svenbro 1994:21n21.

words *weft* or *woof*, there is also *web*. In a marked sense, *web* is a synonym of *weft* and *woof*. In an unmarked sense, however, *web* designates simply 'fabric' as an entirety, consisting of both warp and weft. Similarly in Latin, *têla* in a marked sense means 'warp'; in an unmarked sense, however, *têla* designates 'loom' as an entirety, consisting of both warp and weft. French *trame*, as we have seen, is the *weft* or *web*; metaphorically, however, it means the *plot* of a narrative.

The metaphor implicit in French *trame* brings us back to the metaphor of weaving as applied to the craft of the singer of songs. As the metaphor of *trame* implies, you cannot have a plot in a story, a horizontal weft, if you do not have a framework to begin with. That framework is the loom, which must start with a vertical warp, which in turn makes possible the horizontal weft. Further, from the standpoint of working at the loom, you cannot start the horizontal weft without first attaching the vertical warp from the cross-bar. The English word *web*, as we have seen, can mean the entire fabric by default, not just the horizontal weft, but that entirety still depends on the warp to start it off. Similarly, the Latin word *têla* may mean the entire loom, not just the vertical warp, and the horizontal axis of the weft depends on the vertical axis of the warp to give it a frame. Let us apply here the Prague School construct of a horizontal axis of combination interacting with a vertical axis of selection. From the standpoint of working at the loom, you cannot move horizontally from one point to the next unless each given oncoming point has already been set for you vertically.

Here I return to my thesis, that the idea of *weaving*, just like the idea of *humnos*, is connected with the idea of *beginnings*. The essential point is the *point of departure*. Wherever you begin, you must have a continuum that follows. Or, in Aristotelian terms, you must have a *consequent*. Here we see the essence of Aristotle's idea of *order* (Greek *sustasis*). The whole-ness of the performance is authorized by the beginning. To repeat, *arkhê* is both beginning and authorization.

Aristotle's idea of *order* in the plot of, say, a tragedy, is comparable to the meaning implicit in the Latin word from which English "order" is derived, *ôrdô*. Also comparable is the meaning of other related Latin words, especially *ôrdior* and *exôrdior*.[31] Each of these Latin words is connected to the metaphorical world of weaving, and each is preoccupied with the idea of beginnings.[32] Here I give just one example of *ôrdior*, showing the implicit meaning of 'start':

> *prisci oratores ab Ioue optimo maximo … orsi sunt*

The ancient orators took their start [*ôrdior*] from Jupiter Optimus Maximus.

Valerius Maximus 1.pr.

In this Latin example, we see a direct parallel to the Greek notion of the *prooimion*:

> ὅθεν περ καὶ Ὁμηρίδαι ῥαπτῶν ἐπέων τὰ πόλλ' ἀοιδοὶ ἄρχονται, Διὸς ἐκ <u>προοιμίου</u>...

starting from the very point where [*hothen*] the *Homêridai*, singers [*aoidoi*] of sewn-together [*rhapta*] utterances [*epê*], most often take their start [= verb *arkhomai*], from the <u>proem</u> [<u>*prooimion*</u>] of Zeus'...

Pindar *Nemean* 2.1–3

---

[31] I elaborate on all these Latin words in another work, N 2000b.

[32] Ernout/Meillet *DELL* s.v. *ôrdior* think that the idea of 'begin' evolved from a "rapprochement" of *orior* and *ôrdior*. The idea of 'begin' is already implicit in the mechanics of weaving on a single-beam warp-weighted loom, so that the idea of 'begin' as conveyed by *ôrdior* is independent of its formal similarity with *orior*.

The *prooimion* 'proem' is to the *oimê* 'thread' (and, probably, the *oimos*) as the *humnos* (as in a Homeric Hymn) is to the rest of the performance, as conveyed by the expression *metabêsomai allon es humnon* 'I will switch to the rest of the *humnos*'. We may note the spondaic *prooimion* of Terpander (PMG 698):

Ζεῦ πάντων ἀρχά, πάντων ἀγήτωρ,
Ζεῦ σοὶ πέμπω ταύταν ὕμνων ἀρχάν

> O Zeus, beginning [/authority] of all things, leader of all things!
> O Zeus, to you do I send this the beginning [/authority] of *humnoi*.

There is a striking parallel in Latin: *cum semel quid orsus, [si] traducor alio, neque tam facile interrupta contexo quam absoluo instituta* 'once I have started weaving [*ordior*] something, if I get distracted by something else, it is not as easy for me to take up where I left off [*contexô*] than to finish what I have started' (Cicero *Laws* 1.3.9).

These metaphors inherent in *humnos* and related words are also pertinent to another phenomenon in the mechanics of weaving on single-beam warp-weighted looms. This phenomenon concerns *starting bands,* that is, *heading bands = starting borders = starting edges.* Here are two useful descriptions:

> "The starting edge is a closed one, and often is quite different from any of the other three edges of the cloth."[33]

> "Heading bands occur in several examples and varieties, but seem always to be of the most sophisticated type: a

---

[33] Barber 1991:271.

tightly woven strip about a dozen threads wide, through which the warp has been pulled in long loops."[34]

The Greek word that we may translate as 'heading band' is *diasma* (cf. *exastis* 'selvedge'). In Hesychius, *diasma* is glossed as *phareos arkhê*, that is, 'the beginning of the fabric'.[35] So also, I propose, the specially intricate *humnos* is the beginning of the rest of the song.

In light of this imagery of heading bands, let us reconsider a form of ancient Greek poetic composition known to modern scholars as the "rhapsodic hymn," featuring aporetic questions that are used "to point up the difficulty of finding a suitable beginning."[36] The prime example is to be found in the *Homeric Hymn to Apollo*, verses 19 and 207:

πῶς γάρ σ᾽ <u>ὑμνήσω</u> πάντως <u>εὔυμνον</u> ἐόντα;

For how shall I <u>hymn</u> you, you who are so absolutely-<u>well-hymned</u>?[37]

The absoluteness of the god's authority is coextensive with the absoluteness of the *humnos*.

---

[34] Barber p. 134.

[35] Barber p. 271. See also Barber 1992:109 on the *diasma* as the *warp*.

[36] Race 1990:104.

[37] Koller 1956:197 argues that this rhetorical gambit at *H.Apollo* 19 / 207, coming as it does after *khaire* / *khairete* (14 /166), which is a gesture that bids the god to reciprocate the pleasure that he has experienced from what has been said to him so far, is a substitute for another gambit, that is, the gesture of a metabasis or 'switch' to the consequent, to the rest of the song. To repeat the earlier argument: the expression *metabêsomai allon es humnon* at verse 293 (cf. *HH* 9.9, 18.11) means not, as is commonly thought, 'I will switch to another *humnos*' but rather 'I will switch to the rest of the *humnos*'. I suggest that the aporetic question is intended to lead to a new beginning — as an alternative to a smooth transition to the consequent.

This notional absoluteness of the *humnos* can be connected, I will now argue, with the ideological authority of Homeric poetry as it evolved in the context of the Feast of the Panathenaia in Athens. In terms of my argument, such an authority was expressed by way of equating this poetry, the *Iliad* and *Odyssey*, with the idea of *humnos*. It is as if the entire corpus of Homeric poetry were the notional equivalent of a single continuous—and gigantic—*humnos* performed for the goddess Athena on the occasion of her Feast, the Panathenaia.

A key to my argument is the cultural mentality that Plato is putting to work for his own philosophical purposes in one of his most admired masterpieces, the *Timaeus*. In the previous chapter, I have examined the indirect historical evidence provided by the *Timaeus* about the rhapsodic traditions of Homeric performance at the Panathenaia of Athens. Here I review only those aspects of my overall argumentation that bear on the metaphorical world of the *humnos*.

The dramatized occasion of Plato's *Timaeus* is 'the sacrificial festival [*thusia*] of the goddess' (τῇ ... τῆς θεοῦ θυσίᾳ 26e3), that is, the Panathenaia.[38] The would-be epic of Atlantis and Athens, about to be narrated by the figure of Critias, is described by him metaphorically as a *humnos* to be sung as an encomium of the goddess Athena, whose sacrificial festival is the occasion of this so-called *humnos*: to recall the narrative, Critias says, would be a fitting way both to please Socrates 'and at the same time to praise the goddess on the occasion of her Festival in a righteous and truthful way, just as if we were <u>making</u> her the subject of a <u>*humnos*</u>' (καὶ τὴν θεὸν ἅμα ἐν τῇ πανηγύρει δικαίως τε καὶ ἀληθῶς οἷόνπερ ὑμνοῦντας ἐγκωμιάζειν 21a2–3).

Precisely in this context, *Timaeus* 20e, Plato evokes the first sentence of Herodotus, the so-called "prooemium" of the

[38] Brisson 1982:38.

History. I repeat what I have just quoted, this time in its larger context, and then I juxtapose it with the wording of Herodotus:[39]

πρὸς δὲ Κριτίαν τὸν ἡμέτερον πάππον εἶπεν,... ὅτι μεγάλα καὶ θαυμαστὰ τῇσδ' εἴη παλαιὰ ἔργα τῆς πόλεως ὑπὸ χρόνου καὶ φθορᾶς ἀνθρώπων ἠφανισμένα, πάντων δὲ ἓν μέγιστον, οὗ νῦν ἐπιμνησθεῖσιν πρέπον ἂν ἡμῖν εἴη σοί τε ἀποδοῦναι χάριν καὶ τὴν θεὸν ἅμα ἐν τῇ πανηγύρει δικαίως τε καὶ ἀληθῶς οἷόνπερ ὑμνοῦντας ἐγκωμιάζειν.

He [= Solon] said to Critias my grandfather ... that there were, inherited by this city, ancient deeds, <u>great</u> and <u>wondrous</u>, that have disappeared through the passage of <u>time</u> and through destruction brought about by human agency. He went on to say that <u>of all these deeds, there was one in particular that was the greatest</u>, which it would be fitting for us now to bring to mind, giving a delightful compensation to you [= Socrates] while at the same time rightly and truthfully praising [*enkômiazô*] the goddess on this the occasion of her festival, just as if we were <u>making</u> her the subject of a *humnos*.

Plato *Timaeus* 20e–21a

Ἡροδότου Ἁλικαρνησσέος ἱστορίης ἀπόδεξις ἥδε, ὡς μήτε τὰ γενόμενα ἐξ ἀνθρώπων τῷ χρόνῳ ἐξίτηλα γένηται, μήτε ἔργα <u>μεγάλα</u> τε καὶ <u>θωμαστά</u>, τὰ μὲν Ἕλλησι, τὰ δὲ βαρβάροισι ἀποδεχθέντα, ἀκλέα γένηται, <u>τά τε ἄλλα καὶ</u> δι' ἣν αἰτίην ἐπολέμησαν ἀλλήλοισι.

This is the public presentation of the inquiry of Herodotus of Halicarnassus, with the purpose of bringing it about that whatever results from men may not, with the passage of <u>time</u>, become evanescent, and that <u>great</u> and <u>wondrous</u> deeds—some of them publicly performed by Hellenes, others by barbarians—may not become things without glory [*kleos*]; <u>in particular</u>,[40] [this presentation concerns] what cause made them war against each other.

Herodotus, prooemium

Plato's evocation of the first words of Herodotus' *History* refers not so much to the beginning of a history per se but to the formal conventions of this beginning.[41] The initial words of Herodotus' history, by virtue of functioning as a *prooimion* 'prooemium', are modeled on the conventions of beginning an epic, not of beginning a "history" per se.[42]

It is important for my argument that Plato evokes the *prooimion* of a grand narration in the same context where he equates the idea of a *humnos* for Athena at the Panathenaia with his own grand narration in the *Timaeus*, which is to be followed by his *Critias*. The narration by Critias of a would-be epic about Athens and Atlantis will have to wait until the *Critias* of Plato gets under way. In the *Timaeus* of Plato, which has to come before the *Critias*, the narration concerns the cosmogony that must precede the would-be epic.

In Plato's rhetorical strategy, we see a confirmation of the traditional homology between *humnos* and *prooimion*. We may find further confirmation in the usage of Thucydides, for whom the *humnos* as a genre is the equivalent of a *prooimion*, as we see

---

[40] The construction here is analogous to Plato's rhetorical device of saying, in effect, "one [superlative] example out of many potential examples."

[41] *PH* 226.

[42] *PH* 215–221.

from his explicit reference (3.104.3–4) to the *Homeric Hymn to Apollo* as a *prooimion* 'prooemium'.[43] For Thucydides, the performance of a Homeric *humnos* is evidently the same thing as the performance of a Homeric *prooimion*. From the standpoint of archaic poetic diction, the difference is that the word *prooimion* refers exclusively to the beginning of a Homeric performance, whereas *humnos* can refer optionally to the whole performance—not only the *prooimion* but also the epic that extends from it.

Pursuing the idea that Homeric poetry, as it evolved, was equated notionally with a *humnos* for the Panathenaia, I need to emphasize that this poetry was not the only tradition that we see evolving within the larger context of the complex institution known as the Panathenaia. The festival of the Panathenaia itself was also all along evolving in its own right.

It is difficult for us to maintain a diachronic perspective on the Panathenaia, just as we find it difficult to do so for the Homeric poems. To get our bearings, we may start by briefly reviewing the main features of this festival as reported in the Aristotelian *Constitution of the Athenians* 60.1–3:

(1) competitions in *mousikê*;[44] prizes awarded: gold and silver.
(2) competitions in athletics, including equestrian events (horse-racing and chariot-racing); prizes awarded: Panathenaic amphoras containing olive oil.
(3) Panathenaic Procession (*pompê*).
(4) presentation of a woven robe, the Peplos, to Athena at the climax of the Panathenaic Procession.

For the moment, I have kept this outline at a minimum, recapping as closely as possible the main features as reported in the

[43] See *PP* 62.
[44] See Ch. 2, where I argue that it is misleading to translate τὸν ἀγῶνα τῆς μουσικῆς in Aristotle *Constitution* 60.1 as "musical competitions."

Constitution (where they are ordered differently, however: 3, 1, 2, 4), and omitting details that are not directly spelled out by the report. One of these omitted details is an essential fact that we know independently from other sources, such as Plato's *Ion*: a prominent feature of the competitions in *mousikê* (no. 1 in the listing above) was the performance of the Homeric *Iliad* and *Odyssey* by rhapsodes.[45]

As we read the Aristotelian *Constitution of the Athenians*, the authoritative picture that we form in our minds can easily become so definitive that we start to lose sight of the fact that the Panathenaia, as described in this report, is different in many ways from earlier and later cross-sections of the same institution. For example, as we take a second look at the description, we notice that the author views the Panathenaia primarily in terms of the elected officials who were responsible for organizing the festival in his own day, the *athlothetai*. And yet, from a diachronic point of view, the function of these officials is clearly a variable:

> The title of the athlothetae suggests that their original duty was to organise the contests (most of which took place at the Great [= quadrennial] Panathenaea only); when the Lesser [= annual] Panathenaea was reorganised in the 330's the procession at that festival was the responsibility of *hieropoioi* [*IG* II^2 334.31–35]; and we may guess that originally [*hieropoioi*] had overall control of the Great Panathenaea, with the athlothetae responsible simply for the contests.[46]

We will return in due course to the variations, over time, in the responsibilities of the *athlothetai*. For now, however, I propose to shift the emphasis from variables to constants in the

---

[45] Again, Ch. 2.
[46] Rhodes 1981:670.

evolving institution of the Panathenaia. A central constant is the *woven robe* or Peplos of Athena, as prominently mentioned by the Aristotelian *Constitution* in the above outline of responsibilities assigned to the *athlothetai*. This Peplos was the "raison d'être" of the Panathenaic Procession as well as the "high point" of the whole Panathenaic Festival.[47] In what follows, I propose to connect the cult object of Athena's Peplos with the concept of the *humnos* that is being notionally created for the purpose of celebrating the goddess on the occasion of the Panathenaia in Plato's *Timaeus*.

The most important day of the Panathenaia was the 28th of the month of Hekatombaion, Athena's birthday.[48] That was the day of the Panathenaic Procession. The climactic ritual presentation to Athena was the cult object of the Peplos. It started being woven nine months earlier, and the time frame matches symbolically the period of gestation before the birth of the goddess.[49]

For essential background, we need to appreciate the ritual significance of the formal presentation of the Peplos to Athena on the occasion of her "birthday" at the climax of the Panathenaia. Further, we have to consider the overall setting of this ritual act of presentation—the acropolis in general and the Parthenon in particular.

It becomes even more difficult for us to maintain a diachronic perspective on the Panathenaia when we stop for a moment to contemplate the representations of this festival in the sculptural art of the Parthenon, looming atop the acropolis of

---

[47] Neils 1992:26.

[48] See Rhodes 1981:693 on the fluctuation between the 28th and the 27th of Hekatombaion. See also ibid. on the day of the month for the birthday when it was celebrated for the "Lesser" (annual) Panathenaia. Rhodes p. 670 says that the Lesser Panathenaia also had a procession, "but at this time [that is, in the era when the Aristotelian *Constitution of the Athenians* was composed] it was only at the Great [= quadrennial] that a new peplos was taken in procession and given to the priestess of Athena to clothe the cult statue." Rhodes also points out that the procession is mentioned for the Lesser in *IG* II 334.

[49] Scheid/Svenbro 1994:27n43.

Athens. Even in its present fragmentary form, the Parthenon stands out as the ultimate synchronic classical statement—as the definitively authoritative testament to the "golden age" of Pericles and to classicism itself. As we consider the sculptures of the temple as an ensemble, we must of course give pride of place to the colossal gold and ivory statue, no longer extant, of the goddess Athena by Pheidias. Even more important for our present purposes, however, are the sculptures of the pediments and metopes on the Parthenon, featuring a set of connected mythical and ritual themes that served to define, in global terms, the Olympian gods in general and the goddess Athena in particular, who embodied the totality of her city of Athens. The east and the west pediment showed respectively the birth of Athena and her victory over Poseidon in their struggle over the identity of Athens; the metopes showed the battle of the gods and giants on the east side, of the Hellenes and Amazons on the west, of the Lapiths and Centaurs on the south, and of the Achaeans and Trojans on the north. I draw special attention to the battle of the gods and giants, with Athena fighting in the forefront as a *promakhos*,[50] and to the Trojan War, the topical centerpiece of the Homeric *Iliad* and *Odyssey*.[51] In terms of my overall argument, these two sets of themes are appropriate respectively to a grandest *prooimion* and a grandest epic, where *prooimion* and epic connect with each other into one single continuous and seamless *humnos*.

Most important of all for our present purposes, the porch colonnades of the Parthenon featured not the expected metopes but instead a continuous frieze extending along the entire length of the outer walls of the cella. What was represented on this Parthenon Frieze was the Panathenaic Procession, which climaxes in the presentation of the Peplos to Athena: "This moment

[50] On the role of Athena in this myth as the central aetiology of the Panathenaia, see especially Pinney 1988.

[51] On which see Pinney 2000.

of handing over the peplos, folded and with its ribbed edge [= selvedge] clearly shown, appears to be depicted on the east frieze of the Parthenon."[52]

The ritual drama of the Panathenaic Procession, as represented on the Parthenon Frieze, is central to the whole Panathenaiac Festival, central to Athena, central to Athens. It is an ultimate exercise in Athenian self-definition, an ultimate point of contact between myth and ritual. The dialectic of such a Classical Moment has us under its spell even to this day. And it is precisely the anxiety of contemplating such a spellbinding moment that calls for the remedy of objective observation, from diachronic as well as synchronic points of view.

As I write, controversy persists over whether or not the Parthenon Frieze—obviously also known as the Panathenaic Frieze—depicts the woven robe or Peplos of Athena realistically.[53] The debate centers on various attested references to a gigantic Peplos that was featured as the sail for an official "ship of state" float that highlighted the parade of the Panathenaic Procession (see especially Plutarch *Life of Demetrius* 10.5, 12.3).[54] The question is, how do we reconcile these references with the other references to the Peplos as the dress for the wooden cult statue (*xoanon*) of Athena?[55] One expert estimates that "the peplos needed to be roughly 5 [feet] by 6 [feet]" in order to dress (literally) this statue.[56] There is an ongoing debate about whether or not to differentiate between the "sail-peplos" of the Panathenaic parade and the "dress-peplos" presented to the cult statue of the goddess. I will not enter that debate here. Instead, I simply draw attention to the observation that the images on the

---

[52] Barber 1992:113; see also Barber 1991:272, with illustration and commentary.

[53] See Barber 1992:114–115, with bibliography. I am planning to publish further on this subject, suggesting modifications to Barber's conclusions and offering supplements to her existing bibliography.

[54] Barber 1992:114, with further references.

[55] Ridgway 1992:120–123.

[56] Barber 1992:114.

Peplos feature "the *same* sacred scene, the Battle of the Gods and the Giants."[57] From here on, I will refer to this all-important scene simply by way of its traditional Athenian designation, *gigantomakhiai* (as in Plato *Republic* II 378c; I note in passing the use of the plural by Plato).[58]

The imagery of *gigantomakhiai* brings us back to the *athlothetai* of the Panathenaia, as described in the Aristotelian *Constitution of the Athenians* (60.1–3). The *athlothetai*, as the description makes clear, were directly in charge of the all activities concerning the Panathenaia, including the supervision of the making of the Peplos (60.1: *kai ton peplon poiountai*); moreover, they were in charge of approving the *paradeigmata* or 'models' of the patterns to be woven into the Peplos (49.3).[59] Those woven patterns were functional narrations of the "sacred scene" of the *gigantomakhiai*, and the technique of representation in such patterns has aptly been described by one expert as the "story-frieze" style of weaving.[60] This responsibility of the *athlothetai* in supervising the narrative woven into Athena's robe is surely relevant to the function of the Peplos as the "raison d'être" of the Panathenaic Procession as well as the "high point" of the whole Panathenaic Festival.[61]

So the obvious question imposes itself: why would such important elected state officials be held responsible for the narrative agenda of the "story-frieze" patterns on the Peplos of Athena? Clearly, these explicit narrative agenda must have matched in importance the implicit political agenda of the State.[62]

---

[57] Barber 1992:114. Italics mine.

[58] On the Peplos and the *gigantomakhiai* woven into it, I find the discussion of Pinney 1988 indispensable (especially p. 471).

[59] Rhodes 1981:671–672. For bibliography on the interpretation of *paradeigmata* here as referring specifically to the patterns on the fabric, see Rhodes p. 568.

[60] Barber 1992:114–116.

[61] See again Neils 1992:26.

[62] There are also some isolated historical occasions when the political agenda were featured explicitly, not just implicitly, on the Peplos itself: see again Plutarch *Life of Demetrius* 12.3; also Diodorus 20.46.2.

We get a sense of this importance directly from the words of Plato, describing the story patterns on the Peplos of Athena:

οἷα λέγεταί τε ὑπὸ τῶν ποιητῶν, καὶ ὑπὸ τῶν ἀγαθῶν γραφέων τά τε ἄλλα ἱερὰ ἡμῖν καταπε-ποίκιλται, καὶ δὴ καὶ τοῖς μεγάλοις Παναθηναίοις ὁ πέπλος μεστὸς τῶν τοιούτων ποικιλμάτων ἀνάγεται εἰς τὴν ἀκρόπολιν

… such things as are narrated by poets, and the sacred things that have been pattern-woven [*katapoikillô*] for us by good artists;[63] in particular the Peplos at the Great [= quadrennial] Panathenaia, which is paraded up to the Acropolis, is full of such pattern-weavings [*poikilma-ta*].[64]

Plato *Euthyphro* 6b–c

The represented speaker here is Socrates, who has just remarked that the public resents him for being skeptical about various myths; he then cites as the first object of his skepticism the central myth of the Athenian State, the Battle of the Gods and Giants, as represented on the Peplos of Athena herself. The all-importance of this myth is marked here not only by the Peplos itself but also by the occasion that highlights the Peplos, that is, the Great [= quadrennial] Panathenaia.

I draw attention to the metaphor of *poikilia* 'pattern-weaving', which establishes a parallelism between poetry and

---

[63] I note with interest the usage of *grapheus* here in the general sense of 'master of the visual arts', not necessarily a 'painter' (as in Plato *Phaedo* 110b). For the use of *(en)graphein* to indicate the weaving-in of patterns, see for example the scholia vetera to Aristophanes *Knights* 556.

[64] For reasons that emerge as the discussion proceeds, I translate *poikillô* as 'pattern-weave' rather than 'embroider' and *poikilmata* as 'pattern-weavings' rather than 'embroidery'.

fabric-work as prime media of mythmaking.[65] Similarly in Plato *Republic* II 378c, the expression *muthologêteon* 'to be mythologized' is made parallel to *poikilteon* 'to be pattern-woven', and the subject of mythologization / pattern-weaving is none other than the battles of gods and giants, that is, the *gigantomakhiai* of the Great Panathenaia.[66]

For the wording, we may compare *Iliad* VI 294, with reference to the *poikilmata* on the great Peplos that Theano the priestess of Athena (VI 300) and the Trojan women offer to the cult statue of Athena at Troy by placing the robe on the goddess's knees (VI 303). These *poikilmata* are "probably woven ... rather than embroidered."[67] Similarly, the story-patterns narrating the Achaean and Trojan 'struggles' (*aethloi*) that Helen 'sprinkles into' (*em-passô*) her web at *Iliad* III 126 are "woven into the cloth and not embroidered on afterwards."[68] Another example is the web of Andromache at XXII 441, which is 'sprinkled' (again, *em-passô*) with patterns of *throna*; this word means 'patterns of flowers'.[69] We may compare the infinitely varied patterns of flowers woven into the robe of Aphrodite *poikilothronos* in Sappho 1.1.[70]

In this context, I focus on a particularly interesting detail: the Peplos destined for dedication to the cult statue of Athena is described as shining like an *astêr* 'star' at *Iliad* VI 295, just one verse after its description as 'the most beautiful' and 'the most big' of all *peploi* by way of its *poikilmata* (VI 294: ὃς κάλλιστος ἔην ποικίλμασιν ἠδὲ μέγιστος). We learn from Aristotle[71]

---

[65] Cf. Plutarch *Life of Pericles* 12.6, with reference to professional pattern-weavers (*poikiltaí*) employed for Pericles' building projects.

[66] See Scheid/Svenbro 1994:27n47, who adduce the Aristotelian *Constitution of Athens* 49.3 in this context.

[67] Kirk 1990:199, relying especially on Wace 1948.

[68] Kirk 1985:280, again relying on Wace 1948.

[69] Cf. Kirk 1985:280.

[70] *PP* 101.

[71] Aristotle F 637 ed. Rose p. 395, via the scholia to Aristides p. 323 ed. Dindorf.

that the Lesser [= annual] Panathenaia were aetiologized in terms of Athena's killing of a Giant named *Asterios*[72] or *Astêr*.[73] The name, especially in the second version, is striking: the Giant is simply 'star'.[74] We may compare again the Peplos dedicated to Athena at *Iliad* VI 295, which shines like an *astêr* 'star'. There is some speculation that this Iliadic simile had motivated the name of the Giant (*Astêr* or *Asterios*).[75] I suggest, rather, that the simile and the name are both cognate with a traditional iconographic narratology of star-patterns woven into the Peplos of Athena at the Great Panathenaia. These stars are telling their own story.[76]

As we contemplate the grand Athenian State narrative of luminous *poikilmata* woven into the Peplos of Athena at the Great Panathenaia, we can appreciate all the more the philosophical magnitude of Socrates' challenge to the central myth of this narrative, the *gigantomakhiai*, in Plato's *Euthyphro* and *Republic*. In effect, Plato's Socrates is challenging the State's definition of Athena and even of Athens itself.

Elsewhere too, Plato uses the aura of the Great Panathenaia to illuminate the importance of his own philosophical agenda. The prime example is our own point of entry into the subject of the Panathenaic Festival, the *Timaeus* of Plato, which equates its own immediate occasion with the ultimate occasion of a festival celebrating the genesis of the goddess who presides over the city of Athens—and which further equates the discourse extending from Timaeus to Critias with a *humnos* to be sung in worship of this goddess.[77] Even further, Plato uses the technical

---

[72] According to one set of scholia to Aristides: Rose p. 395.20.

[73] According to another set of scholia: Rose p. 395.5.

[74] The wording of the second version is of interest: ἐπὶ ᾿Αστέρι τῷ γίγαντι ὑπὸ ᾿Αθηνᾶς ἀναιρεθέντι. On the semantics of *epi* plus dative in contexts of aetiologizing various festivals, see *PH* 121; also 119n15 and 142n38.

[75] Scheid/Svenbro 1994:28n48.

[76] I should add that the stars of Plato's *Timaeus* are in turn telling their own story.

[77] On the interruption of the discourse after it extends from the *Timaeus* to the *Critias* of Plato, see Ch. 2.

language of rhapsodes in conveying the continuities and discontinuities of the discourse extending from the *Timaeus* as text to the *Critias* as text.[78]

Another example is the *Parmenides* of Plato: the setting is again the Great [= quadrennial] Panathenaia (127a), which has just attracted a visit from the luminous Parmenides himself, accompanied by his charismatic friend Zeno (127a). The whole dialogue of the *Parmenides,* featuring the "quoted words" of Parmenides and Zeno and a youthful Socrates (126b–c), is represented as spoken by the character of Kephalos, who says that he heard these words from Antiphon (126b and following), who in turn heard them from Pythodoros, a friend of Zeno's who was present at the occasion of the dialogues.[79] The elusiveness of establishing the "original words" of this dialogue is relevant, I suggest, to the dramatic setting of the Panathenaia, which also serves as the historical setting for the performance of Homeric poetry by rhapsodes.

This dramatized occasion of the dialogue that is the *Parmenides* coincides with a public reading by Zeno of a written text (*grammata*) that he is introducing for the first time in Athens and that the youthful Socrates has been eager to hear (127c). Socrates now hears the whole reading by Zeno. Not so Parmenides and Pythodoros, who are late in arriving and miss most of the reading (128c–d). A detail is ostentatiously added at this point: Pythodoros had already heard Zeno perform a public reading on a previous unspecified occasion (128d). When Zeno finishes reading, Socrates asks him to read again the first hypothesis of the first argument (*logos*), and this re-reading becomes the point of entry for the dialogue to begin, with a direct "quotation" of a question by Socrates (128d–e) in response to the re-reading.

By the time this Platonic dialogue gets underway, we have already been given the impression that its words may well

[78] Ch. 2.

[79] For background on this narratological framing, see Hadot 1983:126n74.

be just as textualized as the words of the written text from which Zeno had performed his public reading. Kephalos says that Pythodoros told the dialogue to Antiphon over and over again (126c) and that Antiphon then practiced "remembering" (*apomnêmoneuei*) the dialogue, word for word, over and over again (126c).

As Socrates and Zeno pursue their dialogue extending from Socrates' question, it becomes clear that Zeno's argument, extending from his written text (*gramma*: 128a, 128b, 128c), is meant as a reinforcement (*boêtheia*) of Parmenides' unwritten poetry (*poiêmata*: 128a).[80] A detail is ostentatiously added at this point: Zeno, who is represented as nearing the age of 40, claims that he originally produced his written text when he was still a young man, and that this original written text was then surreptitiously copied and has been circulating as a copy ever since (128d–e). Socrates, Zeno tells him, should accept the uniqueness of the original, not the plurality of the copies (128e). The elusiveness of this "original" text of Zeno, as parodied here by Plato, is analogous to the elusiveness of an "original" text of Homer.

The figure of Socrates replies that he accepts and follows this line of thinking, and in saying so he evokes a technical term conventionally used by rhapsodes to express the connection, by relay, of one performance to the next: the word is *apodekhomai* (128e: ἀλλ' ἀποδέχομαι), which I translate for the moment as 'I accept and continue from here'. As I have already stressed, the *Timaeus* of Plato is full of similar technical references, by way of the word *dekhomai*.[81] For example, when it is Critias' turn in the *Critias* to take up where Timaeus in the *Timaeus* had left off, he says: *dekhomai* (*Critias* 106b: ἀλλ' ... δέχομαι). Timaeus had

---

[80] On the related idea that the written text needs as its own 'reinforcement' (*boêthoos*, *boêtheia*) the living voice of the author or extensions of the author, see Plato *Phaedrus* 275e, 276c8, already discussed in Ch. 1.

[81] See Ch. 2.

just said: 'I hand over [*paradidomen*] to Critias, as prearranged, the continuous discourse [*ephexês logos*]' (*Critias* 106b: παραδίδομεν κατὰ τὰς ὁμολογίας Κριτίᾳ τὸν ἐφεξῆς λόγον). I draw attention here to the expression *ephexês logos* 'continuous discourse', which applies in "Plato" *Hipparkhos* 228b–c to the seamless web of Homeric poetry as performed by rhapsodes at the Panathenaia.[82]

Such metaphors of rhapsodes performing at the Panathenaia in Plato's *Timaeus* and *Parmenides* bring us back one last time to the occasion of the Peplos, which is coextensive with the occasion of performing the *Iliad* and the *Odyssey* in their ultimately authorized setting. That merged occasion is the Great [= quadrennial] Panathenaia. Every four years, the identity of Athens becomes definitively reaffirmed with the official re-weaving of Athena's web and with the official re-performance of the Homeric *Iliad* and *Odyssey*. This quadrennial convergence of Peplos and authorized Homeric performance at the Great Panathenaia is I think the central historical fact to be considered in the search for answers to the ongoing questions about the textualization of Homer.

My own ongoing question remains this: was this re-performance of Homer equated, metaphorically, with the re-weaving of the Peplos? The answer, I have argued, can be found in the metaphor implicit in the usage of *humnos* at *Odyssey* viii 429, as applied to the totality of Homeric poetry.

In the allegorizing commentary of Proclus on the *Timaeus* of Plato, the notional *humnos* of Plato's discourse is interpreted as a Peplos in its own right,[83] more real even than the cult object presented to the goddess every four years by the ancient Athenians.[84] For Proclus, the ultimate Peplos is the web

---

[82] See again Ch. 2.

[83] Proclus commentary ed. Festugière 1966 vol. I p. 122.

[84] Proclus commentary ed. Festugière 1966 vol. I pp. 182–183.

woven by the essence of intelligence, the luminous intellect of Athena.[85] Scholars who study the *Timaeus* in our own time have suggested that Plato himself must have intended this masterpiece of his, this *humnos*, as his very own Peplos for the goddess.[86] I suggest that the metaphor applies also to Homeric poetry, as a Panathenaic *humnos* destined for eternal re-weaving in the eternally self-renewing context of Athena's festival.

We know, of course, that this mentality of re-weaving gives way, in the course of time, to a web no longer re-woven. Once the weaving stops, the web can become a text. Homer can become textualized. The etymology of English *text*, from Latin *textus*, recapitulates the idea of textualization: the metaphor of 'weaving' is still alive in Latin *textus* (from *texô* 'weave'), but it is dead in English *text*.[87] Similarly with Greek *humnos* at *Odyssey* viii 429, the metaphor of 'weaving' dies with the textualization of Homer.[88]

---

[85] Proclus commentary ed. Festugière 1966 vol. I p. 183; cf. Hadot 1983:129.

[86] Hadot 1983:117.

[87] On the metaphorical background of Latin *textus* as 'weaving', see *PP* 65, with further references.

[88] I save for another project my discussion of a related theme: the daily re-weaving of Penelope's web, unwoven the night before (*Odyssey* ii 104–105, xxiv 139–140).

Appendix
Rhapsodes and Actors

As argued in Ch. 1, there are parallelisms in the evolution of *rhapsôidoi* 'rhapsodes' and *hupokritai* 'actors'. Even the terminology referring to rhapsodes and actors is parallel: for example, *theatai* 'theater-spectators' in Plato *Ion* 535d8 refers to the audiences who attend the performances of the rhapsodes. I disagree with Boyd 1994:112, who argues that *Ion* 535d1–5 refers not to epic rhapsodes but exclusively to tragic actors. He offers three points: (1) the performer is pictured as *kekosmêmenos* 'decked out, adorned' with variegated clothing and with a golden wreath [d2] during performance, although Ion has yet to win first prize at the Panathenaia; (2) the occasion of the performance is described as a *thusia* 'sacrifice' [d3], and he claims that "there is no evidence of rhapsodic performance at sacrifices"; (3) it is not clear *where* a rhapsode could perform before an audience as large as 20,000 people.

On the first point, Boyd himself observes (p. 112n8) that Socrates later on in the *Ion* imagines the rhapsode as wearing a golden wreath (541b8–c2), and that this wreath may well be what Ion won as first prize at the festival of the Asklepieia in Epidaurus (cf. 530a3–4). I should note that competing rhapsodes may have been allowed to wear wreaths that they had won in earlier competitions. As Socrates is represented as saying elsewhere in the *Ion* (530b6–7), rhapsodes are expected to be "decked out," *kekosmêsthai*, for their competitions. Perhaps the simplest solution, however, is that Plato's Socrates proleptically imagines Ion as a victor—before the rhapsode actually wins first prize at the Panathenaia.

On the second point, I note that the word *thusia* is attested at line 42 of IG XII ix 189, an inscription from the city of Eretria in Euboea (ca. 341/0 BCE) concerning a festival of Artemis, which features competitions of rhapsodes (lines 10, 15). I elaborate in Ch. 2, where I also argue that the word *thusia* in Plato *Timaeus* 26e2 refers definitely to the Panathenaia.

As for the third point, one possible site for imagining a Panathenaic audience listening to rhapsodic performances of Homer is the Pnyx. (Boyd, p. 113, actually mentions the Pnyx as a possibility.) In Plato *Ion* 535e, Ion describes himself as looking down, from the *bêma* or podium, at a sea of faces in the audience. This description seems to match passages describing speeches in the *ekklêsia* or assembly on the Pnyx, where speakers were raised above their audiences by standing on the *bêma*: see Plutarch *Themistocles* 19.6 and the commentary of Camp 1996:45, who argues that the Pnyx featured this "sermon on the mount" configuration in a period extending from the early fifth century all the way through the "Pnyx III" stage of the fourth century. During that period, as Mogens Hansen points out to me, the average number of citizens actually attending a session of the *ekklêsia* would be around 6,000, even if the body politic is notionally figured at around 20,000.

Later on, under Lycurgus in the 330s, the new Theater of Dionysus could be used for the *ekklêsia* (see Pollux 8.132 and the comments of Camp p. 46). Under Demetrius of Phalerum, who was in power at Athens from 317 to 307, it seems that the Theater could now also be used for Homeric performances (see Athenaeus 620b–c and the comments in *PP* 158–163).

Another possible site for imagining a Panathenaic audience listening to rhapsodic performances of Homer is the Odeum. Plutarch *Life of Pericles* 13.11 links Pericles with the institution of contests in *mousikê* at the Panathenaia (ἐψηφίσατο μουσικῆς ἀγῶνα τοῖς Παναθηναίοις ἄγεσθαι), specifying performances involving the *aulos* and the *kithara* and singing (καθότι χρὴ τοὺς ἀγωνιζομένους αὐλεῖν ἢ ᾄδειν ἢ κιθαρίζειν), and then he goes on to add that such contests were held in the Odeum not only in the era of Pericles but in other eras as well, though he leaves the dating unspecified (ἐθεῶντο δὲ καὶ τότε καὶ τὸν ἄλλον χρόνον ἐν 'Ὠιδείῳ τοὺς μουσικοὺς ἀγῶνας). Plutarch also leaves it unspecified whether the *agônes* 'contests' included rhapsodic performance, but we may infer that they were indeed included if we take into account the report in Hesychius under the entry for "Odeum," where it is specified that the Odeum was the site for contests of rhapsodes and citharodes before such contests were transferred to the Theater (s.v. ᾠδεῖον· τόπος, ἐν ᾧ πρὶν τὸ θέατρον κατασκευασθῆναι οἱ ῥαψῳδοὶ καὶ οἱ κιθαρῳδοὶ ἠγωνίζοντο).

Bibliography

Barber, E. J. W. 1991. *Prehistoric Textiles: The Development of Cloth in the Neolithic and Bronze Ages, with Special Reference to the Aegean*. Princeton.

———. 1992. "The Peplos of Athena." In Neils 1992:103–117.

Becker, A. S. 1995. *A Rhetoric and Poetics of Early Greek Ekphrasis: Theory, Philology, and the Shield of Achilles*. Lanham, Maryland.

Berve, H. 1966. "Vom agonalen Geist der Griechen," *Gestaltende Kräfte der Antike* (2nd ed.) 1–20. Munich.

Boyd, T. W. 1994. "Where Ion Stood, What Ion Sang." *Harvard Studies in Classical Philology* 96:109–121.

Brisson, L. 1982. *Platon: Les mots et les mythes*. Paris.

Camp, J. McK. II. 1996. "The Form of Pnyx III." In B. Forsén and G. Stanton, eds., *The Pnyx in the History of Athens, Papers and Monographs of the Finnish Institute at Athens* II: 41–46. Helsinki.

Canto, M., trans. and commentary. 1989. *Platon: Ion*. Paris.

Carter, J. B., and Morris, S. P., eds. 1995. *The Ages of Homer: A Tribute to Emily Townsend Vermeule*. Austin.

Chadwick, J., and Baumbach, L. 1963. "The Mycenaean Greek Vocabulary." *Glotta* 41:157–271.

Chantraine, P. 1968, 1970, 1975, 1977, 1980. *Dictionnaire étymologique de la langue grecque* I, II, III, IV–1, IV–2. Paris. Abbreviated as *DELG*.

Clay, D. 1997. "The Plan of Plato's *Critias*." *Interpreting the Timaeus–Critias: Proceedings of the IV Symposium Platonicum, Selected Papers*, ed. T. Calvo and L. Brisson, 49–54. Sankt Augustin.

Cook, E. F. 1995. *The Odyssey at Athens: Myths of Cultural Origin*. Ithaca.

Davison, J. A. 1955. "Peisistratus and Homer." *Transactions of the American Philological Association* 86:1–21.

— — —. 1958. "Notes on the Panathenaia." *Journal of Hellenic Studies* 78:23–41 = 1968:28–69.

— — —. 1968. *From Archilochus to Pindar: Papers on Greek Literature of the Archaic Period.* London.

DELG. See Chantraine 1968–1980.

DELL. See Ernout and Meillet 1959.

Detienne, M. 1989. *L'écriture d'Orphée.* Paris.

Dihle, A. 1995. "Platons Schriftkritik." *Jahrbuch der Akademie der Wissenschaften in Göttingen* 1995:120–147.

Dougherty, C. 2001. *The Raft of Odysseus: The Ethnographic Imagination of Homer's* Odyssey. Oxford.

Dougherty, C., and Kurke, L., eds. 1993. *Cultural Poetics in Archaic Greece: Cult, Performance, Politics.* Cambridge.

Dumézil, G. 1984. *"... Le moyne noir en gris dedans Varennes."* Paris.

— — —. 1999. *The Riddle of Nostradamus: A Critical Dialogue.* Translated by B. Wing from Dumézil 1984. Baltimore.

Dunkel, G. 1979. "Fighting Words: Alcman *Partheneion* 63 *makhontai.*" *Journal of Indo-European Studies* 7:249–272.

Edwards, M. W. 1991. *The Iliad: A Commentary. Volume V: Books 17–20* (general ed. G. S. Kirk). Cambridge.

Ernout, A., and Meillet, A. (1959) *Dictionnaire étymologique de la langue latine: Histoire des mots* 4th ed. Paris. Abbreviated as *DELL.*

Festugière, A. J. 1966. *Proclus: Commentaire sur le Timée.* I. Paris.

Figueira, T. J. 1985. "The Theognidea and Megarian Society." In Figueira and Nagy 1985:112–158.

Figueira, T. J., and Nagy, G. 1985. *Theognis of Megara: Poetry and the Polis.* Baltimore.

Flueckiger, J. B. 1996. *Gender and Genre in the Folklore of Middle India.* Ithaca.

Foley, J. M. 1991. *Immanent Art. From Structure to Meaning in Traditional Oral Epic.* Bloomington.

Ford, A. 1988. "The Classical Definition of ΡΑΨѠΙΔΙΑ." *Classical Philology* 83:300–307.

———. 1992. *Homer: The Poetry of the Past*. Ithaca.

Gibson, D. A. 1996. "On the History of a Misunderstanding: The Hymenaios and the Etymology of the *Humên* Refrain." A.B. thesis, Harvard University.

Hadot, P. 1983. "Physique et poésie dans le *Timée* de Platon." *Revue de théologie et de philosophie* 115:113–133.

Hainsworth, J. B. 1988. Commentary on Books v–viii of the *Odyssey* in A. Heubeck, S. West, and J. B. Hainsworth, eds., *A Commentary on Homer's Odyssey*. Oxford.

———. 1993. *The Iliad: A Commentary. Volume III*. Books 9–12 (general ed. G. S. Kirk). Cambridge.

Haslam, M. 1976. "A Note on Plato's Unfinished Dialogues," *American Journal of Philology* 97:336–39.

Heiden, B. 1996. "The Three Movements of the Iliad." *Greek Roman and Byzantine Studies* 37:5–22.

———. 1997. "The Ordeals of Homeric Song." *Arethusa* 30:221–240.

———. 1998. "The Placement of 'Book Divisions' in the Iliad." *Journal of Hellenic Studies* 118:69–82.

Householder, F. W., and Nagy, G. 1972. *Greek: A Survey of Recent Work*. The Hague.

Jacopin, P.-Y. 1988. "Anthropological Dialectics: Yukuna Ritual as Defensive Strategy." *Schweizerische Amerikanisten-Gesellschaft, Bulletin* 52:35–46.

Janko, R. 1982. *Homer, Hesiod and the Hymns: Diachronic Development in Epic Diction*. Cambridge.

———. 1990. "The *Iliad* and its Editors: Dictation and Redaction." *Classical Antiquity* 9:326–334.

———. 1992. *The Iliad: A Commentary. Volume IV*. Books 13–16 (general ed. G. S. Kirk). Cambridge.

———. 1998a. Review of Morris and Powell 1997. *Bryn Mawr Classical Review* 98.5.20.

———. 1998b. "The Homeric Poems as Oral Dictated Texts." *Classical Quarterly* 48:1–13.

————. 1998c. Review of Nagy 1996a. *Journal of Hellenic Studies* 118:206–207.

Jensen, M. Skafte. 1980. *The Homeric Question and the Oral-Formulaic Theory.* Copenhagen.

Kirk, G. S. 1962. *The Songs of Homer.* Cambridge.

————. 1976. *Homer and the Oral Tradition.* Cambridge.

————. 1985. *The Iliad: A Commentary. Volume I.* Books 1–4. Cambridge.

————. 1990. *The Iliad: A Commentary. Volume II.* Books 5–8. Cambridge.

Koller, H. 1956. "Das kitharodische Prooimion: Eine form-geschichtliche Untersuchung." *Philologus* 100:159–206.

Kotsidu, H. 1991. *Die musischen Agone der Panathenäen in archaischer und klassischer Zeit: Eine historisch-archäologische Untersuchung.* Quellen und Forschungen zur antiken Welt vol. 8. München.

Lamberterie, C. de. 1997. "Milman Parry et Antoine Meillet." In Létoublon 1997:9–22. Translated as "Milman Parry and Antoine Meillet" in Loraux, Nagy, and Slatkin 2001:409–421.

Létoublon, F., ed. 1997. *Hommage à Milman Parry: Le style for-mulaire de l'épopée homérique et la théorie de l'oralité poétique.* Amsterdam.

Liddell, H. G., and Scott, R. 1940. *A Greek-English Lexicon* (9th ed., rev. H. S. Jones). Oxford.

Loraux, N., Nagy, G., and Slatkin, L., eds. 2001. *Antiquities* (Postwar French Thought, ed. R. Naddaff, Volume III). New York.

Loraux, P. 1993. *Le tempo de la pensée.* Paris.

Lord, A. B. 1953. "Homer's Originality: Oral Dictated Texts." *Transactions and Proceedings of the American Philological Association* 94:124–134. Rewritten, with minimal changes, in Lord 1991:38–48 (with an "Addendum 1990" at pp. 47–48).

————. 1960. *The Singer of Tales.* Harvard Studies in Comparative Literature 24. Cambridge, MA.

―――. 1991. *Epic Singers and Oral Tradition*. Ithaca.

―――. 1995. *The Singer Resumes the Tale*, ed. M. L. Lord. Ithaca.

―――. 2000. Second 40th anniversary edition of Lord 1960, ed. S. Mitchell and G. Nagy. Cambridge, MA.

Lowenstam, S. 1993. *The Scepter and the Spear: Studies on Forms of Repetition in the Homeric Poems*. Lanham, Maryland.

―――. 1997: "Talking Vases: The Relationship between the Homeric Poems and Archaic Representations of Greek Myth." *Transactions of the American Philological Association* 127:21–76.

LSJ. *See* Liddell and Scott 1940.

Lynn-George, M. 1988. *Epos: Word, Narrative and the Iliad*. London.

Macleod, C. W. 1982. *Homer Iliad Book XXIV*. Cambridge.

Martin, R. P. 1989. *The Language of Heroes: Speech and Performance in the Iliad*. Ithaca.

―――. 1993. "Telemachus and the Last Hero Song." *Colby Quarterly* 29:222–240.

Meillet, A. 1925. *La méthode comparative en linguistique historique*. Paris.

Merkelbach, R. 1952. "Die pisistratische Redaktion der homerischen Gedichte." *Rheinisches Museum* 95:23–47.

MHV. *See* Parry 1971.

Miller, A. M. 1986. *From Delos to Delphi: A Literary Study of the Homeric Hymn to Apollo*. Leiden.

Mitchell, S., and Nagy, G. 2000. Introduction to the Second Edition. In Lord 2000:vii–xxix.

Monro, D. B., and Allen, T. W., eds. 1920. *Homeri Opera* ed. 3. Oxford.

Morris, I., and Powell, B., eds. 1997. *A New Companion to Homer*. Leiden.

Muellner, L. 1976. *The Meaning of Homeric EYXOMAI through its Formulas*. Innsbruck.

———. 1990. "The Simile of the Cranes and Pygmies: A Study of Homeric Metaphor." *Harvard Studies in Classical Philology* 93:59–101.

———. 1996. *The Anger of Achilles: Mênis in Early Greek Epic.* Ithaca.

Murnaghan, S. 1987. *Disguise and Recognition in the* Odyssey. Princeton.

Murray, P., ed. with commentary. 1996. *Plato on Poetry: Ion, Republic 376e–398b, Republic 595–608b.* Cambridge.

Nagy, B. 1992. "Athenian Officials on the Parthenon Frieze." *American Journal of Archaeology* 96:55–69.

Nagy, G. 1974. *Comparative Studies in Greek and Indic Meter.* Harvard Studies in Comparative Literature 33. Cambridge, MA.

———. 1979. *The Best of the Achaeans: Concepts of the Hero in Archaic Greek Poetry.* Baltimore.

———. 1981. "An Evolutionary Model for the Text Fixation of Homeric Epos." *Oral Traditional Literature: A Festschrift for Albert Bates Lord* (ed. J. M. Foley) 390–393. Columbus.

———. 1982. Review of Detienne 1981. *Annales Economies Sociétés Civilisations* 37:778–780.

———. 1990a. *Pindar's Homer: The Lyric Possession of an Epic Past.* Baltimore. Revised paperback version 1994.

———. 1990b. *Greek Mythology and Poetics.* Ithaca. Revised paperback version 1992.

———. 1992a. "Homeric Questions." *Transactions of the American Philological Association* 122:17–60. Recast in Nagy 1996b.

———. 1992b. "Mythological Exemplum in Homer." *Innovations of Antiquity*, ed. R. Hexter and D. Selden, 311–331. New York and London. Recast in Nagy 1996b.

———. 1992c. Introduction to Homer, *The Iliad*, translated by R. Fitzgerald (Everyman's Library no. 60), v–xxi. New York.

———. 1992d. "Authorisation and Authorship in the Hesiodic

Theogony." *Essays on Hesiod* II (ed. A. N. Athanassakis) = *Ramus* 21:119–130.

— — —. 1994–1995. "Genre and Occasion." *METIS: Revue d'anthropologie du monde grec ancien* 9–10:11–25.

— — —. 1994a. "The Name of Achilles: Questions of Etymology and 'Folk Etymology'." *Illinois Classical Studies* 19, *Studies in Honor of Miroslav Marcovich* vol. 2, 3–9.

— — —. 1994b. "The Name of Apollo: Etymology and Essence." *Apollo: Origins and Influences* (ed. J. Solomon) 3–7. Tucson.

— — —. 1994c. *Le meilleur des Achéens: La fabrique du héros dans la poésie grecque archaïque.* Translated by J. Carlier and N. Loraux. Paris.

— — —. 1995a. "An Evolutionary Model for the Making of Homeric Poetry: Comparative Perspectives." In Carter and Morris 1995:163–179. Recast in Nagy 1996b.

— — —. 1995b. Review of Foley 1991. *Classical Journal* 91:93–94.

— — —. 1996a. *Poetry as Performance: Homer and Beyond.* Cambridge.

— — —. 1996b. *Homeric Questions.* Austin.

— — —. 1997a. "Ellipsis in Homer." *Written Voices, Spoken Signs: Tradition, Performance, and the Epic Text*, ed. E. Bakker and A. Kahane, 167–189, 253–257. Cambridge MA.

— — —. 1997b. "Homeric Scholia." In Morris and Powell 1997: 101–122.

— — —. 1997c. "L'épopée homérique et la fixation du texte." In Létoublon 1997.57–78.

— — —. 1997d. "An inventory of debatable assumptions about a Homeric question." *Bryn Mawr Classical Review* 97.4.18.

— — —. 1997e. "The Shield of Achilles: Ends of the *Iliad* and Beginnings of the Polis." *New Light on a Dark Age: Exploring the Culture of Geometric Greece* (ed. Susan Langdon), pp. 194–207. Columbia MO.

———. 1998a: "The Library of Pergamon as a Classical Model." *Pergamon: Citadel of the Gods* (ed. H. Koester) *Harvard Theological Studies* 46, 185–232.

———. 1998b: "Aristarchean Questions," *Bryn Mawr Classical Review* 98.7.14.

———. 1998c. "Homer as 'Text' and the Poetics of Cross-Reference." *Verschriftung und Verschriftlichung: Aspekte des Medienwechsels in verschiedenen Kulturen und Epochen* (eds. C. Ehler and U. Schaefer) 78–87. ScriptOralia 94. Tübingen.

———. 1999a. *The Best of the Achaeans: Concepts of the Hero in Archaic Greek Poetry*. 2nd ed., with new introduction, Baltimore.

———. 1999b. "Homer and Plato at the Panathenaia: Synchronic and Diachronic Perspectives." *Contextualizing Classics* (eds. T. M. Falkner, N. Felson, D. Konstan) 127–155. Lanham, Maryland.

———. 1999c. Foreword. In Dumézil 1999:vii–xi.

———. 1999d. "Epic as Genre." *Epic Traditions in the Contemporary World: The Poetics of Community* (eds. M. Beissinger, J. Tylus, and S. Wofford) 21–32. Berkeley and Los Angeles.

———. 1999e. "Irreversible Mistakes and Homeric Poetry." *Euphrosyne: Studies in Ancient Epic and its Legacy in Honor of Dimitris N. Maronitis* (ed. J. N. Kazazis and A. Rengakos) 259–274. Stuttgart.

———. 2000a. "Epic as Music: Rhapsodic Models of Homer in Plato's *Timaeus* and *Critias*." *The Oral Epic: Performance and Music* (ed. K. Reichl) 41–67. Berlin.

———. 2000b. "Homeric *humnos* as a Rhapsodic Term." *Una nueva visión de la cultura griega antigua hacia el fin del milenio* (ed. A. M. González de Tobia) 385–401. La Plata.

———. 2000c. Review of Martin L. West, ed., *Homeri Ilias. Recensuit / testimonia congessit. Volumen prius, rhapsodias I–XII continens*. Stuttgart and Leipzig: Bibliotheca

Teubneriana, 1998. *Bryn Mawr Classical Review* 00.09.12 (2000), http://ccat.sas.upenn.edu/bmcr/2000/2000–09–12.html

— — —. 2000d. "Distortion diachronique dans l'art homérique: quelques précisions." *Constructions du temps dans le monde ancien*, ed. C. Darbo-Peschanski, 417–426. Paris.

— — —. 2001a. "The Textualizing of Homer." *Inclinate Aurem— —Oral Perspectives on Early European Verbal Culture*, ed. J. Helldén, M. S. Jensen, and T. Pettitt, 57–84. Odense.

— — —. 2001b. "Homeric Poetry and Problems of Multiformity: The 'Panathenaic Bottleneck'." *Classical Philology* 96:109–119.

Neils, J. 1992. "The Panathenaia: An Introduction." In Neils 1992:13–27, plus notes at pp. 194–195. References to Neils 1992 will indicate this chapter.

— — —, ed. 1992. *Goddess and Polis: The Panathenaic Festival in Ancient Athens*. Princeton.

Nilsson, M. P. 1906. *Griechische Feste*. Leipzig.

Olson, S. D. 1995. *Blood and Iron: Stories and Storytelling in Homer's Odyssey*. Leiden.

Parke, H. W. 1977. *Festivals of the Athenians*. Ithaca.

Parry, A. 1966. "Have We Homer's *Iliad*?" *Yale Classical Studies* 20:177–216.

— — —, ed. 1971. *The Making of Homeric Verse: The Collected Papers of Milman Parry*. Oxford.

Parry, M. *See MHV*.

Peradotto, J. 1990. *Man in the Middle Voice: Name and Narration in the Odyssey*. Princeton.

Perpillou, J.-L. 1970. Review of E. Benveniste, *Le vocabulaire des institutions indo-européennes*, 2 vols. (Paris 1969). *Revue des Etudes Grecques* 83:534–537.

Pfeiffer, R. 1968. *History of Classical Scholarship from the Beginnings to the End of the Hellenistic Age*. Oxford.

Pinney, G. Ferrari. 1988. "Pallas and Panathenaea." *Proceedings of the Third Symposium on Ancient Greek and Related*

Pottery (eds. J. Christiansen and T. Melander) 465–477. Copenhagen.

———. 2000. "The Ilioupersis in Athens." *Harvard Studies in Classical Philology* 100:119-150.

Pucci, P. 1979. "The Song of the Sirens." *Arethusa* 4:103–117.

———. 1987. *Odysseus Polutropos: Intertextual Readings in the Odyssey and the Iliad*. Ithaca.

———. 1995. Second edition of Pucci 1987, with a new afterword at pp. 247–258.

Race, W. H. 1990. *Style and Rhetoric in Pindar's Odes*. Atlanta.

Reichel, M. 1994. *Fernbeziehungen in der Ilias*. *ScriptOralia* 62. Tübingen.

Rengakos, A. 1993. *Der Homertext und die hellenistischen Dichter*. Hermes Enzelschriften 64. Stuttgart.

Reynolds, D. F. 1995. *Heroic Poets, Poetic Heroes: An Ethnography of Performance in an Arabic Oral Epic Tradition*. Ithaca.

Rhodes, P. J. 1981. *A Commentary on the Aristotelian Athenaion Politeia*. Oxford.

Richards, I. A. 1936. *The Philosophy of Rhetoric*. Oxford.

Richardson, N., ed. 1993. *The Iliad: A Commentary. Volume VI: Books 21–24* (general ed., G. S. Kirk). Cambridge.

Ridgway, B. S. 1992. "Images of Athena on the Acropolis." In Neils 1992:119–142.

Rousseau, P. 1996. "Διὸς δ' ἐτελείετο βουλή: Destin des héros et dessein de Zeus dans l'intrigue de l'Iliade." Doctorat d'Etat thesis, Université Charles de Gaulle - Lille III.

Rüter, K. 1969. *Odysseeinterpretationen: Untersuchungen zum ersten Buch und zur Phaiakis*. Edited by K. Matthiessen. Göttingen. *Hypomnemata* no. 19.

Rutherford, R. B. 1991–1993. "From the *Iliad* to the *Odyssey*." *Bulletin of the Institute of Classical Studies* 38:37–54.

Saussure, F. de. 1916. *Cours de linguistique générale*. Critical ed. 1972 by T. de Mauro. Paris.

Scheid, J., and Svenbro, J. 1994. *Le Métier de Zeus: Mythe du tissage et du tissu dans le monde gréco-romain*. Paris.

Schmitt, R. 1967. *Dichtung und Dichtersprache in indogermanischer Zeit*. Wiesbaden.

Schrader, H., ed. 1880–82. *Porphyrii Quaestionum Homericarum ad Iliadem pertinentium reliquiae* I–II. Leipzig.

Scully, S. 1990. *Homer and the Sacred City*. Ithaca.

Seaford, R. 1994. *Reciprocity and Ritual: Homer and Tragedy in the Developing City-State*. Oxford.

Shapiro, H. A. 1992. "Mousikoi Agones: Music and Poetry at the Panathenaia." In Neils 1992:53–75, plus notes at pp. 199–203.

— — —. 1993. "Hipparchos and the Rhapsodes." In Dougherty and Kurke 1993:92–107.

Sherratt, E. S. 1990. "'Reading the Texts': Archaeology and the Homeric Question." *Antiquity* 64:807–824.

Stanley, K. 1993. *The Shield of Achilles: Narrative Structure in the Iliad*. Princeton.

Stansbury-O'Donnell, M. D. 1995. "Reading Pictorial Narrative: The Law Court Scene of the Shield of Achilles." In Carter and Morris 1995:315–334.

Taplin, O. 1980. "The Shield of Achilles within the *Iliad*." *Greece and Rome* 27:1–21.

— — —. 1992. *Homeric Soundings: The Shaping of the Iliad*. Oxford.

Verdenius, W. J. 1972. "Notes on the Proem of Hesiod's *Theogony*." *Mnemosyne* 25:225–260.

Wace, A. 1948. "Weaving or Embroidery?" *American Journal of Archaeology* 52.51–55.

West, M. L. 1973a. "Greek Poetry 2000–700 B.C." *Classical Quarterly* 23:179–192.

— — —. 1973b. "Indo-European Metre." *Glotta* 51 161–187.

— — —. 1981. "The Singing of Homer and the Modes of Early Greek Music." *Journal of Hellenic Studies* 101:113–129.

— — —. 1982. *Greek Metre*. Oxford.

— — —. 1985. *The Hesiodic Catalogue of Women*. Oxford.

————. 1990. "Archaische Heldendichtung: Singen und Schreiben." *Der Übergang von der Mündlichkeit zur Literatur bei den Griechen* (ed. W. Kullmann and M. Reichl) 33–50. Tübingen.

————. 1995. "The Date of the *Iliad*." *Museum Helveticum* 52:203–219.

————. 1997. "The Homeric Hexameter." In *The New Companion to Homer* (eds. I. Morris and B. Powell) 218–237. Leiden.

West, S. 1967, ed. *The Ptolemaic Papyri of Homer*. Papyrologica Coloniensia 3. Cologne and Opladen.

————. 1988. "The Transmission of the Text." *A Commentary on Homer's Odyssey. Introduction and Books i–viii* (ed. A. Heubeck, S. West, and J. B. Hainsworth) 33–48. Oxford.

Whitman, C. H. 1958. *Homer and the Heroic Tradition*. Cambridge, MA.

Witte, B. 1964. "Der ΕΙΚΩΣ ΛΟΓΟΣ in Platons *Timaios*." *Archiv für Geschichte der Philosophie* 46:1–16.

Index

I

iambic 55
IG II 2311 38, 39, 42, 51
IG II 334 88
IG II 334.31-35 87
IG XII ix 189 39, 51, 99
IG XII ix 189.10-15 40
IG XII ix 189.1-8 48
IG XII ix 189.39 50
IG XII ix 189.41-42 53
IG XII ix 189.5 39
Iliad
   1.1 27
   1.1-5 63
   1.1ff 74
   1.5 62
   1.292 20, 21
   2.794 26, 72
   3.103 47
   3.126 93
   6.294 93
   6.295 93, 94
   6.300 93
   6.303 93
   8.76 65
   8.470-483 65
   9.79-80 18, 19
   9.184-191 17
   9.189 16
   9.191 10, 60, 61
   12.17-33 66
   13.745 69
   15.14-33 65
   15.49-77 65
   15.494-499 11
   15.600 65
   19.55-73 20
   19.78-144 21
   19.79-80 19, 20
   19.80 21
   19.80 (B scholia) 20
   21.211-327 66
   22.441 93
   23.335ff 23
   23.340 23
   23.657 21

   23.706 21
   23.752 21
   23.760-763 78
   23.801 21
   23.830 21
Iliou Persis 26, 72
inspiration, rhetoric of 25, 26
intentionality, questions of 25, 29, 30,
   59, 67
interlacing, working definition of 76
intertextuality 58, 59
Ion the rhapsode 22, 23, 24, 25, 29, 33,
   34, 35, 37, 55, 99, 100, 101
Ionism 11
Isocrates
   Panegyricus 159 22, 42
   Panathenaicus 24, 30, 31, 33

J

Jupiter Optimus Maximus 80

K

Kephalos 57, 95, 96
Koureotis 54

L

Lapiths 89
Latin
   contexô 81
   exôrdior 80
   harundô 78
   iugum 78
   laudandus 28
   laudator 28
   ôrdior 80, 81
   ôrdô 78, 80
   orior 80
   radius 78
   stâmen 78
   subtemen 78
   têla 78, 79
   texô 'weave' 98
   textus 98